THE QUINTESSENTIAL
GENTLEMAN

THE QUINTESSENTIAL GENTLEMAN

AN IRONIC, SOMETIMES IRREVERENT GUIDE TO 21ST-CENTURY MANNERS

By Henry Russell, Elegant Englishman

Ulysses Press

The author wishes to thank the following
for their help and suggestions:

Sara Jones, Jon Asbury, Jack Angell, Mark Fletcher,
Brian Innes, Vanna Motto, Aruna Vasudevan.

———————————————

First published as *Etiquette: Henry's Guide to Modern Manners*
in Great Britain in 2006 by Cassell Illustrated, an imprint of
Octopus Publishing Group Limited

ISBN10: 1-56975-556-6
ISBN13: 978-1-56975-556-3
Library of Congress Catalog Number: 2006903819

10 9 8 7 6 5 4 3 2 1

U.S. Editors: Nicholas Denton-Brown, Barbara Schultz
Cover design: Diane VanEycke
Cover photograph: ©Royalty-Free/Corbis
Index: Sayre Van Young
Illustration on page 68: Emma Parrish

Printed in Canada by Transcontinental Printing

Distributed by Publishers Group West

To my enemies
(*My friends already know all this*)

*"Let no one say that I have said nothing new:
the arrangement of the material is new."*
Pascal

CONTENTS

INTRODUCTION

*"Never speak disrespectfully of Society....
Only people who can't get into it do that."*

Oscar Wilde, *The Importance of Being Earnest*

Everyone wonders how to behave. Sometimes the questions raised are moral, and in extreme cases the wrong moral decisions can lead to serious trouble. However, most of the problems we routinely encounter are rather less weighty. They are largely matters of what constitutes the right social behavior—what to say and when to say it, whether or not to wear a tie to the office party, whether to call the children's teacher "Mr. Smith" or "John."

These are problems of etiquette. Etiquette receives less consideration than morality because violations are seldom harmful, just embarrassing. Moral misdemeanors, in contrast, can lead to imprisonment or death.

Not all questions of etiquette are entirely trivial. People are usually at pains to ensure that their comments do not cause unnecessary offense to others; they tend to become most anxious when they have to participate in rites of passage, especially christenings, marriages and funerals. As Walter Savage Landor wrote, "More can be said in a minute than can be forgotten in a lifetime."

Nevertheless, with certain exceptions, it is quite proper that most niceties of etiquette should be taken less than completely seriously. A man who ignores someone because he has asked him the location of the "toilet" instead of using his own preferred genteelism for WC is an ass. While we may deprecate those who say "ain't" instead of "isn't," their transgression would not be serious even if there were a law against it.

There was a time when such things mattered more than they do today. Throughout the 18th and 19th centuries, and for the greater part of the 20th century, the observance of etiquette was both a diversion and an occupation, especially for women. More and more rituals were devised to create a sense of exclusivity among initiates. These rituals were later codified and to some extent invented by writers of all sexes. Leaders of fashion and so-called pundits pontificated on the rights and wrongs of dress, cutlery and a host of related trivia. An individual's acceptability in society and, indeed, his entire reputation might have hung not upon his honesty, but upon how he conveyed his soup from bowl to mouth.

In the United States, Emily Post laid down the rules of social behavior in *Etiquette: The Blue Book of Social Usage*. First published in 1922, revised editions appeared regularly for more than 30 years. Among other prominent standard-setters were Amy Vanderbilt, and Eleanor Roosevelt in her *Book of Common Sense Etiquette* (1962).

Prescriptive etiquette reached its nadir in Britain in 1956 with *Noblesse Oblige: An Enquiry into the Identifiable Characteristics of the English Aristocracy*, an anthology best remembered for dividing social behavior into two categories: "upper class" ("U") and "non-upper class" ("non-U"). The former was extolled and the latter deplored. The social impact of this absurd book, edited by Nancy Mitford, may still be felt today: there are, almost incredibly, some circles in which the use of the supposedly "non-U" term "serviette" instead of the supposedly "U" term "napkin" would still arouse adverse comment, and from which anyone using the "wrong" term might find himself excluded.

Most people who live by the precepts of Mitford have now been sidelined, and modern society is better equipped than ever before to keep etiquette in proper perspective. There are several reasons for this healthy development. One is that women are now freer, if not actually liberated, and have more important—or at least more pressing—matters to occupy them. Another is the "anything goes" spirit of the age. There has lately been a welcome rehabilitation of Rabelais' maxim *fay ce que vouldras* (do what you will), which was vilified in the middle of the 20th century as the watchword of a black magician called Aleister Crowley. Children of the sixties then brought it back into favor with the sensible rider "as long as it doesn't harm anyone else."

There are those who believe that this zeitgeist has made etiquette rule books obsolete. Towards the end of 1995, the London *Evening Standard* newspaper boldly announced that "Today…no general etiquette survives, whether of clothes, of speech, or of behavior. Socially, life is a journey without maps. Only style choices remain, and good and bad manners."

But there still are many occasions when we are uncertain of what to do, what to wear, what to say and how to say it. This uncertainty undermines us. The most elaborate premeditated attempts to behave properly may go unnoticed, while the smallest departure from generally accepted standards of behavior arouses derision. Dire offense may spring from the most trivial causes. If, for example, a man eats peas off his knife, the "victim" (if that is not too strong a term to describe someone who happens to have witnessed the petty outrage) may feel aesthetic revulsion; the "culprit," meanwhile, may grow ill-disposed towards the person in front of whom he feels he has made a fool of himself, on La Rochefoucauld's principle that "We may forgive those who hurt us, but never those whom we hurt."

The only serious reason for observing etiquette is to avoid upsetting others. Etiquette is not, or shouldn't be, a weapon in the class struggle, a stick with which to beat those of whom you happen not to like the look or sound. This book gives an outline of what other people expect— not in the sense of "England expects," but in the sense of "presumes most likely to occur."

Readers will avoid embarrassment in their social intercourse only if they treat the information contained here, not as laws, but as reportage of current conventions—conventions which they can observe or flout as they prefer.

If you do something outré unintentionally, onlookers' gasps of astonishment may throw you off your stride; if, on the other hand, you know that your flies are undone and you have left them open deliberately in order to shock or to draw attention to yourself, you may be looked upon not as provincial or beyond the pale but as a style guru. In the words of the Trummy Young/Sy Oliver song, "'T ain't what you do, it's the way that you do it." Still, while iconoclasts make their own rules, most of us prefer to familiarize ourselves with established conventions and stick to them.

The purpose of good behavior is to make everyone— yourself and those around you—feel at ease. And what, as Norman Douglas asked, are good manners but the outward expression of kindliness? And what is kindliness but common sense?

Henry Russell

GENERAL
BEHAVIOR

Just as some people feel they can't face the evening without a stiff drink, there are others who cannot engage in any form of social or business interaction without a preconceived idea of what they're going to say and what they must avoid mentioning. This book is not on the whole prescriptive; what follows are mostly suggestions, not instructions. It stakes various premises, but acknowledges that we live in a pluralistic society. The reader may care to venerate its tenets as holy writ, or alternatively do the opposite of everything it suggests. If you find it diverting, it will have achieved its modest purpose.

❦

BELCHING

Burping happens. If you can't hold a belch in, simply say "Excuse me," and carry on as if nothing went wrong. Do cover your mouth, and don't blow your noxious fumes into the faces of others.

❦

CONVERSATION

" Questioning is not the mode of conversation among gentlemen. "

Samuel Johnson, *Boswell's Life*

If we go by what we read, we are not supposed to discuss politics, money, religion or sex in polite company. Which leaves art, and since no one knows anything about that, what is left? Nothing. If in doubt, let the host and hostess be responsible for setting the tone, and take it from there. If you are running the show, start off as trivially and uncontroversially as you can and see what develops.

Remember that it is bad form to leave someone standing on his own, and it is reprehensible to leave someone all evening with a known bore. If you find that you're frequently left with bores all night, either you're going to the wrong parties or you're a bore yourself.

Conversation Starters

One not-too-leaden way to start a conversation with someone you don't know is to talk about an external event or phenomenon about which he might also have an opinion: the difficulty of finding the venue, the traffic en route, a painting on the wall. You might even open with the weather, but only if it is extreme and you are desperate. Asking the other person how he knows the host is not a bad opening gambit. In any case, remember that you are supposed to be introducing a light topic for discussion, not trying to sustain a soliloquy until the dinner gong is sounded. Conversation is to some extent like tennis—when you are serving, if the first ball is not returned, put another one in play. (But don't stretch the metaphor too far...for every ace you lose a point.)

Age

Never ask someone else's, and never ask others to guess yours. If you are asked to guess someone else's, it is politic to subtract at least five years from what you really think, unless you have been asked to guess by a teenager, in which case it is advisable to add a year or two. Under-tens are impressed only if you get their age exactly right.

Bores

At times you may find yourself trapped by an indefatigable bore who insists on telling you an anecdote for the fiftieth time. You might try to put him off by saying "Yes, that's a lovely story," but even if you're brave enough to do that, you may still not be able to stop him.

The best way to escape gracefully is to pretend that it is you who are boring them. English poet Robert Browning is said to have concluded an audience with a tedious admirer of his work with: "But my dear fellow, this is too bad. I am monopolizing you." An Oxford professor once dismissed a group of bores (one of whom—let's start off as honestly as we hope to continue—was me) from his presence with: "But I mustn't take up any more of your time." (Note the exact words; "valuable time" would have been obviously and insultingly exaggerated.)

Such gambits are witty but risk giving offense, and since perfectly civilized people will always avoid causing pain or embarrassment to others—even at the risk of hurting themselves—the best advice is probably that, if boredom is inevitable, lie back and put on a brave face.

"Every hero becomes a bore at last."

Ralph Waldo Emerson, *Representative Men. Uses of Great Men*

Compliments

Everyone loves to be complimented, but only as long as there is neither a hint of equivocation nor ambivalence. English playwright Alan Bennett took the view that—so numerous are the pitfalls—the only thing you can possibly say to the cast backstage after a performance is "Marvelous, marvelous, marvelous." If you pay compliments that can be construed as backhanded, don't be surprised when they are.

If you're going to praise, you must praise everything. If you do not, it may be interpreted as an implicit criticism of something else you haven't mentioned. Thus for example, it may be advisable to thank your hostess for a wonderful evening: if you say it was a lovely meal, it may be taken to suggest that you didn't like the wine or the company.

Eye Contact

When people are speaking to you, maintain eye contact with them and give them cues (nods, grunts of assent, etc.)

that show that you are listening and engaged. This doesn't mean that you stare at them with large, unblinking eyes. That would be creepy. Your job is not to stare holes into their heads, but to encourage them to continue (assuming you want them to continue, of course).

When you are speaking, you should also seek eye contact with your audience. The speaker has more rein, however, to break his gaze away from the listener periodically.

Gambling

There is no such thing as a dull subject, and in the hands of a good narrator both the theory and practice of gambling may be riveting. Many people, however, make the mistake of expecting the audience to believe that they have come out ahead over a lifetime. Few habitual gamblers are net winners: those who tell you they have "won big" in Vegas have almost certainly excised from their memory the dozen losing trips that put them out of pocket overall.

How Do You Like It Here?

If people ask you this, bear in mind they may be natives. If they are, it is certain that they want you to gush. So that's what you should do, particularly in New York and Tel Aviv,

---

GREAT QUESTIONS OF OUR TIME

In 1978 British broadcaster David Frost conducted a series of interviews with Richard Nixon. Frost later recalled that, on resuming recording after a break in the schedule, the first thing Nixon said to him was: "Did you do any fornicating over the weekend?" Despite the authority of presidential usage, such questions should not be asked; indeed, it would be better not to speak at all.

---

every native of which seems to think he hewed his birth-place from the living rock himself. So even if you've just been mugged on the subway or spent five hours at an army checkpoint, say something positive.

I was once asked that question by a Frankfurter, and although my private view was that the city is not the most immediately admirable jewel in the crown of industrial Germany, I replied that I thought it was lovely. But my inter-locutor persisted: "In what way? What do you particularly like about it?" I told her that it reminded me of Geneva. She looked happy, but still not satisfied. "How is it like Geneva?" I had no option but to tell her that they both had a lot of banks. We have not maintained a vigorous correspondence.

Personal Criticism

If you make disparaging remarks about A to B, what con-fidence can B have that you won't say the same things about him to C? On the other hand, if you don't express any opinions, conversation is impossible. You may be able to convey disapproval in honeyed terms but it takes work to achieve.

Personal Questions

In addition to "How old are you?" and "What do you do?" it is wise to avoid "Was it anything serious?" And for the same reason: the answer may be embarrassing. Likewise, avoid asking "How much do you earn?" While it may be amusing and sometimes instructive to ask that straight out, there are good reasons for not raising such a sensitive sub-ject. First, the most likely reply is either "Mind your own business" or the demurely veiled alternative "I'm not telling you that." Neither encourages further discourse. If the

---

LITERARY CRITICISM

If you're going to talk about literature, feel free, but avoid at all costs the following words and expressions. They are either pretentious or meaningless (or both).

It's effective

Riffing on themes of biography (or anything else)

Ballsy high-octane prose

The human condition

It works on several levels

Definitive statement of the relation of art to life

Evocative

Objective correlative

---

question happens to evoke a numerical response, the conversation has drifted into dangerous territory. The sum of money mentioned will probably be incredible: if you earn that much, how come you drive only a budget car; if you earn so little, how come you have a vacation home in Aspen? As they say in American sitcoms: don't go there.

> *"Although there exist many thousand subjects for elegant conversation, there are persons who cannot meet a cripple without talking about feet."*
>
> Ernest Bramah, *The Wallet of Kai Lung*

Quotations

These should be used only when they are fully relevant in context; otherwise they sound like something you prepared

---

SOCIAL SITUATION

In conversation at a party someone tells you that he admires Monet's *Water Lilies*. How should you respond?

A) Ask him if he loves the work because he wishes he could paint that well himself.

B) Suggest that he is psychologically debilitated by the realization that he will never create anything as good.

C) Tell him your own response to the work, or say something witty and/or interesting about the artist, or bring the subject round to another topic about which you know something.

Answer: (c) Why do people assume that appreciation of art is a reflection of the personality of the observer? One of art's main attractions is that it is apart from the self.

---

before you came out and were going to use, come hell or high water. And, of course, it's important to be word-perfect lest a stickler set you straight.

"'When a book and a head come into contact and one of them sounds hollow, is it always the book?'

'Schopenhauer's line, isn't it?'

'Yes, but it is easier to write a line than to remember it at the perfect moment.'"

Ben Hecht and Charles MacArthur, *The Scoundrel*

Work

Some etiquette authorities proscribe talking about one's own work and asking other people about theirs. Others quote Oscar Wilde, "It is very vulgar to talk about one's business. Only people like stock brokers do that, and then merely at dinner parties." But this is a line in *The Importance of Being Earnest*, not a Mosaic Law. "What do you do?" is likewise frowned upon and regarded as contemptibly trite, but generally what else is there to say?

If you use this line, you must be prepared for all the possible answers. A 19-year-old male friend addressed it to a lady in a short skirt and fishnet tights as she sat on a Soho barstool. To which she answered: "I work, like everybody else."

You may be able to carry it off, if you say it in a mildly ironic tone meant to convey your awareness that, although it's a corny line, contrived situations call for contrived measures.

Some common replies to "What do you do?" typically are followed by an awkward silence and require quick thinking on the part of the interlocutor. They include: "Not a lot," "Housewife," "Accountant" and "Insurance adjuster." Forewarned is forearmed, so think of a suave reply to each.

You can always break the ice by being controversial, but this takes courage and skill. You must ensure that you're not being inflammatory and you must never be tactless.

Never be deterred from saying something on the grounds that everyone will have heard it already. Remember the epigraph of this book: "Let no one say that I have said nothing new: the arrangement of the material is new." Never think no one will be interested in "little old me." If you are truly polite, you will always be too busy thinking of others to have any time to be inhibited by your own self-consciousness.

"*The question 'What do you do?' means*
'How do you earn your living?' On my passport
I am described as a 'Writer'; this is not embarrassing
for me in dealing with the authorities, because immigration
and customs officials know that some kinds of writers make
lots of money. But if a stranger in the train asks me my occupation,
I never answer 'writer' for fear that he may go on to ask me
what I write, and to answer 'poetry' would embarrass us both, for
we both know that nobody can earn a living simply by writing
poetry. (The most satisfactory answer I have discovered, satisfactory
because it withers curiosity, is to say Medieval Historian.)"
W. H. Auden, *The Dyer's Hand*

X Marks the Spot

Don't ask people directly how they intend to vote or have
voted in a political election. In the civilized world the bal-
lot is secret, and their choice is between them and their
conscience.

~

FLATULENCE

Everyone passes gas. It is a natural part of the human condition. Of course, no one *wants* to break wind in
respectable company, but if you let one slip simply say
"Excuse me," and continue your conversation as naturally
as possible. If you are on the receiving end of a fart, do not
sneer or draw attention to the fact. If the culprit has any

sense of self-consciousness, he will be embarrassed enough without your rubbing his nose in it.

If you pass gas without sound, you'll have to make a quick judgment call (silent and deadly or silent and innocuous). If you believe it's the latter, say nothing and no one will be any the wiser. If it's the former, either say "Excuse me," once the smell permeates, or walk briskly to the nearest exit. If you walk fast enough you should be able to drag your stink with you.

GROOMING

Unless you are going for the calculated bohemian hipster look, you should, at a minimum, shower, shave, brush your teeth, and comb your hair every morning before you leave the house. With the advent of metrosexuality, however, it is becoming much more acceptable for a man to go several steps beyond these basics to include eyebrow plucking, hair styling, and nose-, ear- and chest-hair trimming. You choose what level of grooming you are comfortable with, but do remember that woman has loved man since the dawn of humanity, which, at last check, predates metrosexuality by several thousand years.

MONEY

People who know how to behave in the presence of money—their own or anyone else's—hold the master key to etiquette and success. Saint Paul, despite devoting his life to disputation and courting controversy, managed in his writings to express some ideas with which it is hard to disagree. Among his least contentious statements was that:

"The love of money is the root of all evil. "

(First Epistle to Timothy, 6:10).

Borrowing and Lending

*"Life, they say, is give and take.
Why never take? "*

Norman Douglas, *Looking Back*

"Neither a borrower nor a lender be" comes from *Hamlet*, and it is such good advice that it is one of the abiding mysteries of drama that Polonius, who says the line, almost always is portrayed as a bore or a buffoon.

Borrowing is best avoided because it can place intolerable strain on a relationship. If you must borrow, try not to ask for anything that you wouldn't lend if it were yours.

Although many people display books on shelves in the common parts of their homes, guests should be at pains to remember that, despite any appearances to the contrary, they are not in a lending library. If you are sufficiently interested in a book to want to borrow it, mention your interest, but allow the host to suggest that he lends it to you. Do not ask.

Where money is concerned, refusal to lend is often less offensive than the acrimony that may be caused by attempts to get it back. If you must lend money to a friend, prepare to lose both it and him. In fact, a cash advance is probably the politest and most effective way of getting rid of someone you don't really like. Debt causes discomfort, and often the debtor will come to hate those from whom he has borrowed.

"O, my fortunes have Corrupted honest men."

William Shakespeare, *Antony and Cleopatra*

Extra Tickets

From time to time a friend may offer you tickets to some event that he is unable to attend himself. If you want the tickets, for pity's sake, offer to pay. I once had tickets to the Men's Final at Wimbledon that I was compelled at the last minute to pass on to a friend. A few weeks after the event, my friend said to me "I really must give you something for those tickets." As I was trying to think of a none-too-pennypinching way to advise her of the printed price of $150, she handed me a five.

Inheritance

If someone comes into money or property, it is tactless to congratulate him on his good fortune; the windfall has come from a tree that the beneficiary will probably have cultivated and may also have loved.

Going Dutch

This is a mad convention in which every member of a group pays for his own share of the bill. Going Dutch aggravates the condition it is designed to alleviate—morbid concern about money. This is because it always affects those who do it in one of two ways: either they hold back on what they order, or else devour as much as possible to get their money's worth. If you must go Dutch, make sure that you divide the total bill by the total number of people. Adding up who had what is intolerable, as you spend more time paying for the food than eating it.

Some people insist on splitting the bill when they go out as a couple. There are many good reasons for wanting to do this, but it is still better to pay for alternate meals than to spend ages sorting out cash and credit cards and scrabbling around for the right change. It is preferable for the host to ask his guest to pay for the whole meal next time. (However, if neither of you can ever remember who last picked up the tab and you have to make notes in your diary to remind yourself, it's time to let the good practice fall into disuse.)

Paying

Pay discreetly and, if possible, not in front of your guests. Do not carry a wallet with dozens of sections that cascade like a plastic waterfall to reveal all your credit cards. Do not say to your companion: "I need to add a tip: what's 15 percent of $200?"

Speaking of Money

It may be unwise to say that you cannot afford something if you are within earshot of anyone who earns—or thinks he earns—less than you, because if that person is of a covetous nature he will assume that anyone richer than he himself can afford anything. He will therefore conclude that you are a miser. And anyway, "afford" is defined by the speaker.

Tipping

Tips are important to the livelihood of service industry workers, most of whom, according to reports, derive more than half their income from gratuities. Employers pay these

---

WHAT DO YOU CALL THAT THING IN YOUR POCKET?

Never refer to money by any diminutive or pet name—it is tasteless and implies that you are so infatuated with it that, although you want to talk about it all the time, you are too bashful to refer to it directly. The only doubtful case is that of "shekel," which may be permissible, but only if you are talking about the modern currency of Israel. The following are some of the words that you should strike from your vocabulary.

Bank	Gelt
Benjamins	Greenbacks
Bread	Mazuma
Bucks	Moolah
Dough	Wad

---

workers low wages because tipping is expected. If they did not earn gratuities, it would be little better than slave labor, so you should pay the extra as a matter of routine.

Restaurants

In restaurants, since service is almost never included in the final bill, you should tip the table waiter or waitress at least 15 percent. (Altogether, that is: if you have two or more flunkies dancing attendance, you don't have to tip them separately.) You could go as high as 20 percent if you've had particularly careful attention, or it if makes a round number, or if indeed you can't do the other math.

Bars

If you are served at a bar or counter, you should aim to leave about 10 percent of the bill, but never less than 50 cents.

Beauty Salons and Barber Shops

Hairdressers and barbers should be tipped a token amount if your hairdresser or barber is not the proprietor of the shop. The amount should be between 10 and 15 percent, but more importantly, it should be the same each time you return to the same individual. Do not "grade" each haircut or alter the amount of your tip, which may lead the hairdresser to assume his or her service is better some times than others. If someone else washes your hair, tip him or her a dollar or two.

Car Washes

At a car wash, you should put a dollar in the cup that is strategically positioned near the exit.

Coatrooms

If you check your coat in a coatroom and are not charged for the service, tip the attendant one dollar.

Deliveries

Delivery people who bring take-out food or groceries should be tipped a dollar or two each time.

Hotels

In hotels, do not routinely tip the concierge unless he provides some special service, in which case you should leave between $10 and $20. If you have room service, tip the waiter 15 percent of the bill. You do not need to tip the chamber maid, unless you have stayed for a long time, in which case leave one dollar for each night.

Porters, Skycaps and Bellhops

Porters, skycaps and bellhops normally receive $1 for the first bag or two, plus a further 50 cents for each additional luggage item.

Shoe Shines

Shoe shine people should get 50 cents to a dollar.

Taxis

Taxi drivers expect 15 percent; ten percent, though less than generous, is not derisory.

Valet Parking

Valet parking attendants expect at least a dollar or two when they return your car.

> *"Ninotchka: 'Why should you carry other people's bags?'*
>
> *Porter: 'Well, that's my business, Madame.'*
>
> *Ninotchka: 'That's no business. That's social injustice.'*
>
> *Porter: 'That depends on the tip.' "*
>
> Ninotchka

SOCIAL SITUATION

You are in a restaurant; your host asks if you want an after-dinner drink. You're not sure if you should accept: he may be testing you to see if you're a boozer; he may not have one himself, and you may not want to drink alone; you may even be worried that he cannot afford it. What should you do?

Decline. Then if he orders one for himself it is safe to assume that if he can afford one he can afford two, so tell him you've changed your mind. A good host will sense a guest's inhibitions and put the offer in another way: "I'm going to have a brandy. Can I interest you in something?"

AT THE MOVIES

The rules are simple. Turn off your cell phone. Do not talk once the previews begin. Leave your seat only when necessary. Do not fondle or make out with your date. If you must eat or drink, do it as noisily as you would if you were in a foxhole under enemy fire. You should not be a part of anyone else's dramatic experience: do unto others as you would have them do unto you.

POSTURE

People judge each other by their posture. They shouldn't but they do. Too slouchy equals a lack of confidence and achievement. Too fluffed up equals arrogance and overcompensation for some hidden deficiency. But an upright person with head high, stomach in, and shoulders back, demonstrates confidence and self-respect—qualities attractive to friends, lovers, and employers alike.

THE SPORTING LIFE

At the Gym

Re-rack your weights. Wipe down your machine. Do not use more than one station at a time unless you are willing to allow others to work in with you. Do not ogle yourself in the mirror (this is tacky—if a gentleman is attractive, he knows it without having to remind himself through constant rein-forcement). Do not attempt to impress a member of the opposite sex with the quantity of weight you can lift. (We are not cavemen and you will only end up hurting yourself.)

Pick-Up Games

Pick-up games are a great, casual way to get some exercise in a team sport. Basketball is usually the sport of choice, though you can find pick-up games for soccer, ultimate frisbee and football. There are some common courtesies:

- Ask the players awaiting their turn "Who's got next?" If their team is not full, ask if you can join them.
- If there's a dispute over who's playing, shoot for it. First one to make it is on.
- Call your own fouls (do you see any refs?), but do not call anything soft or marginal that didn't drastically alter the flow of the game. Nothing will have you sitting on the sidelines faster than being labeled as the guy who calls ticky-tack fouls.

At a Sports Event

Do not stand unless everyone else is standing around you. The people behind you paid for their seats and have every right to enjoy the view from them.

Try to combine your trips to the restroom/beer vendor/hot dog stand, so that the people in your row don't get a quad workout from sitting and standing every time you have to pass by. The fans came to watch athletics, not perform them.

When slipping by people in your row to get to your seat, face those seated so you can keep your eyes on a potential assailant who might push you over the edge either delib-erately or because he's a clumsy oaf.

If someone in your row orders something from one of the food-hawkers roaming the stands, you are expected to pass money down one way and return the chosen item and any change the other way.

If you are rooting for the away team, do not cheer over-exuberantly and be respectful of the home team. This is less for reasons of etiquette than for personal safety.

AT THE THEATER OR A LIVE PERFORMANCE

Although one of the main reasons for attending any artis-tic performance—drama, music, standup, magic, or what have you—is to make judgments about it, do not impose your opinions. It should go without saying that other members of the audience don't want to know what you think while the show is on. The same goes for the intermissions: have you ever noticed that the validity and interest of a person's critical insights are normally inversely proportional to the volume at which he broadcasts them?

Also remember to turn off your cell phone, arrive in time to be seated before the performance begins, and, once seated, leave only when necessary.

FORMS OF
ADDRESS

One of the most basic rules of etiquette is to get other people's names and titles right. Forgetting them altogether may be excusable, if only on grounds of senility, but calling Darren "Darwin" is invariably insulting. What goes for personal contact also applies to written communication. In a letter there is no better way of turning honey into vinegar than by getting the name or title of the addressee wrong. If you need to write to an official and you are in doubt about his name and/or full title, first call his office to check.

ADDRESSING PEOPLE

"One of the hassles in life is that no one understands the difference between a viscount and a lord."

Viscount Thurso

Bosses

Although there are still some companies where managers are addressed as Mr. this or Ms. that, most employers today cultivate an unbuttoned, casual image and insist that everyone calls them by their first names. Such informality may shade into the kind of friendliness that induces a faint sensation of nausea in staff and outside observers alike.

Doctors

Only doctors of medicine should be addressed as "Dr." It is pretentious and a lapse of taste for doctors of anything other than medicine (such as PhDs) to expect to be so described. The most famous non-medical doctor was Goebbels.

Elected Officials

In England social precedence is clearly marked out, but in the United States the pecking order is less codified, though it is strongly adhered to in some circles. At the head of the list comes the incumbent President, followed by the Vice President, the Speaker of the House of Representatives, the Chief Justice of the United States and any former Presi-

HONORING THE DEAD

Use "Mr." and "Miss," "Mrs." or "Ms." only for people who are alive. This precept should be observed particularly in literary essays: if you refer to "Mr. Chaucer" or "Miss Austen" you suggest they're still with us; "Chaucer" and "Austen" should convey the idea that they're not composing but decomposing. Similarly with honors—if you talk about the work of Sir Terence Rattigan, you should strictly be referring only to those works the dramatist wrote after he was knighted. Now that he's passed away you can avoid tying your prose in knots by just calling him Rattigan. There are customary exceptions to this rule, however: one is the poet Sir Thomas Wyatt, who has retained his title ever since his death in 1542; another is Sir Arthur Sullivan (ob. 1900).

dent. All high-ranking officials tend to be called "Sir" or "Ma'am" (rhymes with "ham"). Letters to the President should be addressed to "The President." The greeting should be "My Dear Mr. President," the valediction "Respectfully yours" or "Sincerely yours." In person, the President should be addressed as "Mr. President" the first time, and then as "Sir." Although former presidents retain their title, there is nothing wrong with newspaper journalists and broadcasters referring to "former President Clinton," because to continue to call him President in almost any context would be misleading. He should still be addressed as Mr. President, however.

Members of the House of Representatives, senators, mayors and governors should be addressed by their title and last name. Judges should be addressed as "Judge" and their last name or as "Your Honor."

Miss

This is a courtesy title for women who are unmarried or operating in a professional capacity in which for a number of reasons they may prefer to use their maiden names. It is now widely superseded by the preferable "Ms."

Mister

If you ask someone his name, assume if he gives a one word answer that that is his surname. Gentlemen do not call themselves "Mister," they leave it to others thus to address them.

Ms.

There is no reason for a woman to make any public declaration of her marital status. Men don't have to. Some people object to "Ms." on the grounds that it contains no vowel sound, but the benefits that derive from the use of the term more than outweigh this. If you're unsure whether a woman is married or not, using Ms. will cause no offense.

ARE YOU TALKING TO ME?

I have from time to time had occasion to reveal my name to trades people of a certain station—let us call them for want of a better generic term "estate agents"—and they have proceeded to call me "Russell." Not wishing to be transported back to school, I have then been forced to point out the error of their ways. Natural breeding or inhibition (take your pick) has prevented me from saying "Actually it's Mr. Russell," so I say "Actually it's Henry Russell." And then they call me Henry, which isn't what I want either.

Priests and Nuns

If you are writing to a Roman Catholic priest, you should style him "The Reverend Father O'Flynn" on the envelope, and start the letter "Dear Father O'Flynn"; you should address him in person as "Father."

The same principles apply to an abbess: respectively, "The Reverend Mother McColl," "Dear Mother McColl," and "Mother." A nun is "Sister."

The valediction of any letter may be as normal ("Sincerely," or whatever); it may also be "Yours in Christ."

Your Children's Teachers

Call them what your children call them. No, wait: call them what your children are meant to call them. If you make the transition to social contact unrelated to school, an instructor may invite you to "Call me Charles," but even so, on back-to-school night it's "Mr. Chipping."

∼

GENERAL CORRESPONDENCE

Care of

A letter is care of ("c/o") a person, but "at" a place. Thus it should be "c/o Joshua Thompson at Pepsi Cola, Inc." Letters to people staying at hotels should be addressed to "John Smith, Hotel Guest, The Sheraton," etc. When writing to a hotel guest, it is helpful to indicate his check-in date on the top left hand corner of the envelope: e.g., "To await arrival February 29."

Christmas Cards

Annual Family Newsletters

Contempt for Christmas circulars—impersonal encyclicals in which families give a round-up of what they've done during the previous year—increases as the practice of sending them becomes more commonplace. Yet it is wrong to condemn them all out of hand because, like any prose work, they can be informative and entertaining if only they are well written. So anyone who can write intelligibly, concisely and with minimal self-regard should not be put off by the ignorant prejudice of others.

Coworkers

Handing out Christmas cards to all your work colleagues is madness, but so many people do it that there is pressure to conform. Either make a point of not sending any yourself, or else bite the bullet; you will at least have the consolation of not having had to pay postage.

No one will think the less of you if you don't send cards at all—provided, of course, that you keep in touch in some other way.

Non-Christians

Non-Christians do not usually worry about receiving Christmas cards, but if you are worried about sending them, choose cards with the messages "Season's Greetings" or "Happy New Year."

Personalizations

It is a nice touch to write the name of the recipient above the greeting on a card; doing so creates the impression that you have taken some trouble over it. However, it is really not good form to write on Christmas cards "We must meet for lunch. Do call to suggest a convenient date." You might as well come right out and say "I'm trying to avoid you." *(See also Answering Machines & Voicemail, page 160.)*

When to Send Them

There are some who maintain that one should send Christmas cards neither too early (in which case it may be thought that one is soliciting a response in order to make one's mantelpiece resemble that of a popular person), nor too late (in case one appears to have only remembered the addressees after receiving their card). Don't worry—just send your Christmas cards whenever you can, any time in December.

Letters

Greetings

The main problems are the greeting and closing. The writer is often unsure whether to address the recipient as "Dear Mr. Smith" or "Dear John." Although it is always better to err on the side of caution and stick to "Dear Mr. Smith," you may like to try "Dear John (may I?)." Alternatively, when writing to people you've met but do not know, you may try the variant "Dear John Smith." Do not address anyone whom you have never met by his forename. Be respectful, never familiar.

Closings

When closing a letter to someone you do not know, you should generally sign off with "Sincerely." A letter to a named person should conclude "Sincerely," unless you know him well enough to use one of the more intimate forms: "Yours truly," "Yours ever," "Best wishes," even "Love." There are no longer taboos about typing or word-processing personal letters unless they're of a particularly intimate nature. Putting the "Dear John" in your own hand is a nice touch.

Man or Woman?

It is not unusual to find that the name of the person you need to contact is sexually indeterminate: Chris Smith could be a man or a woman. If in doubt when writing, use the full name every time; he or she will just have to accept the omission of the usual "Mr." or "Ms." If you're calling, ask for Chris Smith and you should be able to get the sex from the voice. It is also common to find that the name of the person you have been given a note to call is unpronounceable. I recently saw a "Wanted" sign that invited witnesses to ring Detective Inspector Dyche. In this case, you would either have to ask the receptionist for the correct pronunciation or hope that you get through on a direct line which the officer answers with the words: "DI Dyche."

Thank You Cards

Unless you know the host well, you should always write a thank you note after anything but the most informal get-together. The exception is children's parties: you took your brood away at the appointed time (*see Punctuality, page 109*), what more can any reasonable parents expect in the way of gratitude?

Some self-styled authorities on etiquette demand that wedding gifts be acknowledged before the ceremony. The practical problems of this are too daunting to contemplate. Have pity and let the newlyweds leave their thank you letters until after the honeymoon.

From Children

If you diligently send presents to nephews, nieces, grandchildren or godchildren on their birthdays and at Christmas, remember that in turn, it is a solemn part of their traditional duty to put off thanking you until at least a month has elapsed (and even then only in reaction to chilling threats from their parents). It may be that during the intervening period you start to wonder if your gifts got there at all, but you don't want to ring in case it seems too pushy. Console yourself that if you miss one of the great days in their lives or if the parcel gets lost in the mail, they'll quickly be on the phone to you to make sure you're not dead.

The Third Person

Invitations and replies in the third person ("Sir Rufus and Lady Winckler request the pleasure of your company at…"; "Peter Schlemiel thanks Sir Rufus and Lady Winckler…") are on the cusp of fashion; many people still write them, but a growing minority regards the practice as too stiff and formal for the present day.

So neither hope nor fear that you will cause a sensation if you reply using "I" or "We" to an invitation in the third person. However, in cases of doubt, it is probably better to use the third person, taking as your model Gaius Julius Caesar, a country boy who did well for himself and eventually became a god.

~

SELF STYLING

Don't call yourself or describe yourself in writing as "Mr." It's a courtesy title that should be left to others to apply to you.

In general, women should be governed by the equivalent rule, although exceptions may be made in cases where they feel it necessary either to emphasize their marital status or to ensure that they are addressed as "Ms."

DRESS

For most occasions, you know how to dress. You just do. You either copy the general style of your host or produce an idiosyncratic variation on the theme. If you've got a function to attend and you don't know what to wear, don't reproach yourself—it's the responsibility of the person extending the invitation to make the dress code clear. If he hasn't done so, don't hesitate to seek clarification. In the absence of further and better particulars, wear what you feel good in. And if you show up in smart casual to find the other guests in suits, try not to be embarrassed because it's not your fault.

❧

BLACK TIE

The words "black tie" on an invitation mean that a man should wear a black dinner jacket with matching beltless trousers and a black bow tie. The jacket may alternatively be white, but the trousers must always be black. The shirt is normally white with a turned-down collar and a plain piqué front, fold-back cuffs and cufflinks. Some men also wear a black waistcoat and/or a black cummerbund. Socks should be black and preferably made of silk. Shoes are usually plain black but may be patent leather as long as they are not on their first outing—if you need to buy a pair, make sure they're broken in before the night of the dinner. Among the possible variants are frilled shirts, wing collars, braided jackets, velvet jackets, fancy waistcoats, colored cummerbunds and/or "arty" bow ties.

For women black tie is less clear. Any length of dress can be worn, and even a top and skirt or a trouser evening suit are now widely acceptable, as long as they are stylish. Black should be the dominant shade, however.

❧

CASUAL FRIDAYS

These seem to work satisfactorily in some companies, but significant numbers of employees find it excruciatingly difficult to strike a happy balance between the normal sober three-piece and the weekend lycra leotard. If you are an employee, imitate the style of your peers without copying any one of them; and if you're an employer who is contemplating the introduction of Casual Friday, think again.

FOOTWEAR

Unless they are rock stars, men should wear black leather shoes with black or gray suits. Brown leather shoes are generally regarded as too casual for business wear, while suede shoes are seen as bohemian. Two-tone brown and white shoes are known as co-respondent's shoes because they are thought to have been the footwear that would be worn by the sort of fellow who gets named in another man's divorce.

A woman of taste will eschew footwear with heels as high as circus stilts. She will also think twice before wearing sling-back shoes with pants, if only because she is aware that it is deplored in some circles. Some authorities deprecate women wearing patent leather shoes with skirts on the grounds that a man may see the reflection of her underwear on her instep. While researching this book, the author interviewed a dozen men who had spent their adult lives vainly looking for evidence to support this fantastic and wishful nonsense.

HEADWEAR

The old advertising slogan, "If you want to get ahead, get a hat" no longer means much. In most walks of life and social contexts there is no need to wear a hat unless you want to do so or desire protection against the sun, cold or rain.

Some forms of headwear denote status—crowns, miters, chefs' hats—but not even monarchs, bishops and cooks wear them all the time; they are mainly ceremonial.

In general, men should remove their hats when indoors, particularly in church. When greeting someone, the hat should be doffed or the wearer should at least touch the brim.

A hat wearer will traditionally remove his headgear for a passing coffin as a mark of respect, even if he did not know the deceased.

Women often wear hats to weddings, and do not need to remove them in the church, although they may do so if they feel like it.

Mosques and orthodox synagogues are among the very few places in which the head must be covered, but paper yarmulkes or keppels are available at the entrances of the latter for those who have nothing else to wear.

Baseball Caps

Symbolically, a baseball cap can suggest that the wearer has made it in career terms but remains anxious to preserve his cred, even if the street on which he struts it is Rodeo Drive. Among the baseball cap wearers who could afford something better upholstered are Spike Lee, Steven Spielberg and Michael Moore. When it comes to donning and doffing, the rules are the same as those for conventional headwear. Baseball cap wearers sometimes think they're too cool to conform to such stuffy conventions, but unfortunately they thus betray their complete lack of *savoir faire*.

Do-Rag

The do-rag is a piece of cloth, tied at the back, which is used to cover the head. Unless you are African American, do not even attempt to wear one of these. You are not "keeping it real." You will just look foolish and will be mocked accordingly.

JACKETS

At a formal dinner, men should not remove their jackets unless they are specifically given leave to do so by the host. This leave will almost never be forthcoming except on the very hottest day or when the air conditioning breaks down. At a more casual event, feel free to ask your host where you can lay your coat.

LOUNGE SUITS

On an invitation this means that you are expected to wear a two-piece business suit consisting of a matching jacket and skirt or pants. The word "lounge" may raise the hackles of those who have sitting rooms, but it beats "business," which they no doubt regard as an even more vulgar term.

MONOGRAMS

Monograms are always in bad taste, especially when they appear on shirts and cufflinks. However, if they have been engraved or sewn onto a gift from a loved one, you will probably have to wear them in his company if at no other time because to leave them off might cause offense.

PANTS

Women can wear pants most anywhere these days, though in very formal or traditional venues the practice may still be frowned upon. On men, however, they continue to be regarded as obligatory.

SHORTS

Some companies—even those that have no particular dress requirements—frown on men in shorts. Although I would not myself be seen dead at work in anything above the ankle—the office may be a jungle but it's not a safari—I have no problem with people who take a different view. Shorts do, however, tend to arouse adverse comment, and I don't make the rules, I merely report custom and usage and do all in my power to avoid unwanted comments about my legs.

TELEVISION WEAR

Since many people now appear on television—not just as program hosts or talking heads, but to give their expertise in interviews or their opinions in sound bites—they should have some idea of what to wear on air. The importance of

TV DOS AND DON'TS

Do

- Make sure your hair is combed
- Wear plain colors
- Accept any professional offer of make-up, especially for studio interviews

Don't wear

- Black, white or very bright colored clothing
- Patterns, especially fine, regular ones such as herringbone that strobe on screen
- Fussy necklaces
- Badges
- Tie- or lapel pins
- Dangly earrings

appearance is perhaps even greater on television than in real life, because if the viewer decides that you look like an ass, you are an ass, no matter how much eloquence and insight your utterances may contain. And if what you wear distracts the audience from the message, you might as well not have bothered to show up at the studio.

TIES

In current fashion, a tie of normal length is preferable to a bow tie, if only because it conceals the buttons, which—if not exactly repellent—most people would rather not see. It also helps to hide any coffee stains on the shirtfront.

Ascots and Cravats

An ascot is a cross between a tie and a cravat. It is rarely worn today. Unlike cravats, which may be of any color and almost any material, ascots are traditionally made of gray, patterned silk. They are knotted in much the same way as a tie, except that the front is not tucked inside the final loop. They are then fastened with a stickpin or tie tack.

The wearing of ascots is generally confined to white-tie occasions, when they are stylish accompaniments to tailcoats and striped gray trousers. At other events, they are generally perceived as de trop. So, too, are cravats, although some people can carry them off with button-down shirts and blazer or sport jacket.

Bow Ties

The man who can knot his own bow tie on the rare occasions that he needs to wear one is a more imposing figure than the man who feels the need to wear a bow tie every day.

⌒

COME AS YOU ARE

Such a bidding will normally be in an invitation to a party held after work. It implies that, although there is no dress code, you should show up in roughly the sort of clothes that you would normally parade before your employer. Of course, the underlying assumption is that you are a clerical or managerial type who is either habitually besuited or at least "smart" in the conventional sense. If you are a gardener, it does not mean that you don't need to remove your soiled boots. If you're going to "come as you are" straight after a casual Friday, you may want to look at yourself in the mirror before leaving the office. Hosts should think twice before inviting people to come as you are to weekend events because on their own time people might wear anything, and wise men will not wish to open Pandora's wardrobe.

WATCHES

Digital watches that beep on the hour should be avoided unless wearing one is essential to one's occupation. Those who wear them to the theater are making the ultimate *faux pas*. And really, who needs a watch anymore, now that cell phones with built-in clocks are ubiquitous?

Jewel-encrusted watches are almost stylish but can look as if they have been dragged into reality from a costume drama. They impress, but they make their wearers appear to be trying too hard. It's as if a watch like this were an alternative to a personality rather than a reflection or extension thereof.

WHITE TIE

Today, "white tie" seldom appears on wedding invitations. It means that men should wear a black or gray tailcoat, black or gray pants with double braid down the outer seam, and a stiff-fronted shirt with detachable wing collar fastened with mother-of-pearl or gold studs and cufflinks. Both waistcoat and bow tie are white pliqué. Shoes and socks are as for Black tie. You can add a black silk top hat, white kid gloves, a black cloak and a black silver-topped cane ad lib.

For women, white tie is less specific. In general it is taken to mean the most glamorous affordable ball gown, the showiest and perhaps even most expensive jewelry, and long gloves with bracelets over them. The gloves should only be removed for eating; shake hands with them on.

FOOD AND DRINK

If we are completely self-assured, embarrassment will not be a consideration: we will neither feel it nor cause it. Yet confidence may be undermined by the unfamiliar. Like many other animals, we are most vulnerable while feeding. How can we make witty remarks while we're struggling to get the bones out of the mackerel or fretting about the correct use of the implement on the table next to the lobster that looks like something from a museum of medical history?

The following pages attempt to signpost a safe route through the dinner table minefield, leaving the reader free to enjoy the meal and the conversation rather than worry about the potentially disastrous social consequences of misusing cutlery and comestibles of which he has no previous experience.

BREAD

Victorian etiquette seems to have been that bread slices should be exactly one and a half inches thick. Today, bread at mealtimes may come any way you like it; preferably, there will be an unlimited supply, but it should always be available on demand.

The important things to remember at a formal dinner are, first, that the bread on your side dish should be broken up with the hands, not cut with a knife. Second, that you should put on the spread—be it butter, caviar, pâté or terrine—little by little, in bite-size portions. Do not spread a large sheet of toast in one fell swoop. Do not break bread over or into the soup.

COFFEE

After-dinner coffee may be served either at the dining table or in the sitting room. Many people are now off "real" coffee, because they find that caffeine keeps them awake at night, so decaffeinated coffee, tea and/or herbal tisanes should also be offered.

CUTLERY

The most important purpose of cutlery is to convey food from bowl or plate to mouth; all other rules about which implement should be used for a particular food are affectation. Having said that, there remain several conventions:

1) Do not eat anything with a spoon that you can eat equally well with a fork. If you are going to mop up sauce, do it with your bread.

2) Do not eat anything off your knife. There are no exceptions to this rule.

3) Never use an item from your own place setting as a serving implement.

4) If the soup bowl has a plate underneath it, the spoon should be placed on the plate rather than in the bowl when you have finished eating.

5) If an item of cutlery is set on the table before you but you don't need it, don't use it. Start with the outermost implements and work inward, course by course. When you have finished, put knife and fork together in the middle of the plate in a "half past six" position. If you drop any cutlery and there are staff waiting at table, don't pick it up; allow them to bring you a replacement. If they are attentive and doing a good job, they should notice at once. If they don't, ask for it, but don't bother to explain why you need it.

6) If you talk with your hands, put your cutlery on the plate while doing so, ideally in the "twenty to four position," but practically anywhere other than at "half past six," which will lead anyone observing your progress through the meal to the conclusion that you've finished.

7) While the cutlery for the preliminary and main courses will be laid to the left and right of the dish, the fork and spoon for the dessert will ordinarily be placed above the "north pole" of the plate. When eating the dessert, use both the implements provided, or else just the fork; do

not use the spoon alone. Why not? you may ask. Don't ask, no one knows—it is probably because that's the way children eat, and the ultimate aim of every sophisticate is to demonstrate that he is not a child.

Chopsticks

Chopsticks are usually provided in Chinese, Japanese, Korean, Thai and Vietnamese restaurants throughout the world. Use them if you like, but do not hesitate to ask for knife, fork and spoon if they are what you prefer. The staff may think you're a hick, but their disapproval is part of the reason you chose to go there.

Fish Knives

Fish knives have been derided since the mid-1950s. They were originally introduced by the Victorians because steel cutlery was supposed to affect the flavor of the fish and only silver would do. But how do you account for their silly shape? They are best avoided, but if they do appear on the table at a dinner party, they're regrettable rather than a gaffe. If you want to show historical awareness, you might serve fish with two forks (that's how the British royal family still eats it), unless you are afraid that your guests may think you've run out of knives.

DIFFICULT FOODS AND EATING WITH THE FINGERS

Some foods are served with special implements to make eating them less unsightly and embarrassing. But there are

---

SOCIAL SITUATION

We once had vegetarian guests for whom my wife created one of the finest lentil bakes in the history of gastronomy, in addition to, and separate from, the flesh that she set before the resident meat eaters. As we picked up our knives and forks, one of the vegetarian visitors asseverated: "I don't know how you can put that muck in your mouths." Guess what we did.

We just kept smiling and never invited them back.

---

many other tricky foods that you are expected to tackle with nothing more than the usual cutlery or with the bare hands alone.

Here are some hints on how to deal with various foods on social occasions.

Apples

No matter how we might eat this fruit in normal circumstances, at a dinner party we should cut it into quarters or eighths with a knife, which is then used to remove the remaining pieces of core and the pits. Alternatively, if you want to remove the skin, make an incision near the top of the fruit and work the knife downward in circles. If you can get the peel off in one piece, it'll look stylish, always assuming that anyone is watching. Then cut into pieces as previously described. Either way, eat what's left with the fingers.

Artichokes

Each leaf should be pulled off and the white tip then dipped in the sauce provided. Do not eat the ends you've been holding, but pile them at the side of your plate.

Asparagus

Pick up the white end, dip the green end in the butter sauce and make every effort not to get it all over your clothing on the way to your mouth. You may sometimes even see silver-plated asparagus holders; you may ridicule them as much as you like, but only on the way home afterward.

Bananas

Everyone knows how a banana should be eaten, but at dinner parties it is expected that you will peel it by hand, slice it with a knife and then eat the pieces with a fork. Why a fork should be used on a dryish banana when oranges are supposed to be eaten with bare hands is anyone's guess. Debrett's *New Guide to Etiquette & Modern Manners* even suggests making the first incision into the banana skin with a knife, but that's a bit mad unless you are unlucky enough to get one of those rare bendy ones that are about as impenetrable as a bank vault.

Caviar

May be and sometimes is eaten with the fingers, although it's pretentious to do so. Better to spoon a small quantity onto your plate and then spread it on toast, which is the only accompaniment it needs.

Cheese

Don't take all the thin or sharp end (the nose) of the cheese, because that's where most of the taste and goodness are supposed to gather, and to do so is looked upon as the height of selfishness. Eat the rind if you like it; if you don't, cut it off and leave it on the side of your plate. Never cut around the rind on the serving plate.

Chicken Wings/Drumettes

Chicken wings or drumettes are too difficult to eat with a knife and fork. Use only one hand partly in order to avoid comparisons with a medieval European despot, and partly to avoid messing up both sets of fingers. In a perfect world chicken wings would be accompanied by a fingerbowl, but in the real one you'll usually have to rely on your napkin.

Corn on the Cob

Corn on the cob should be held in both hands by its ends, and nibbled as it is rotated. Since this food is almost impossible to eat in a dignified manner, a caring host may think twice about serving it.

Crab

Crab cocktails are easy: eat them with the small fork provided. Claws are more challenging: Break them open with a nutcracker, pull the resulting smaller pieces apart with the fingers, then eat the meat with a fork.

Eggrolls

The correct method of conveying these items from plate to face may be extrapolated from the context. In formal settings, use chopsticks or fork; at lunch with the children, fingers are fine.

Eggs

Gulls' eggs and quails' eggs are served hardboiled. They should be cracked on the side of the plate, peeled, dipped in salt and eaten with the fingers.

Grapefruit

Grapefruit halves are always sectioned before they reach the dinner table, except by practical jokers and sadists.

Grapes

Don't pick a grape or grapes from the serving dish; rather break off a small bunch and eat them with your hands. I have read that in some homes they provide grape scissors, but I have never seen such things, and fear that if I did I might wonder if they had been transferred for the occasion from the bathroom where they were normally used for cutting toenails.

Kumquats

Cut the top off and eat in the hand. Don't embarrass yourself and fellow guests by trying to dissect it with a knife and fork.

Lemons

Lemon should be squeezed with the fingers unless it is a thin slice in which case it should be squeezed between knife and fork.

Lobster

If you get a cold claw, it is quite in order to pick it up and excavate the deepest and tastiest recesses of the crustacean with the special lobster fork that ought to have been provided.

Mussels

Hold the shell in the fingers and extract the contents with a fork. Pile the empty shells onto another plate. Finally, use a spoon to eat the soup at the bottom of the bowl. If a mussel isn't open, don't open it—just move it onto the out-tray.

Olives

Olives are quite straightforward until you come to the pit. The natural and polite method of disposal is to put your

---

EATING JAPANESE CUISINE

- Don't rub your chopsticks together. Doing so implies you're looking for splinters, and is thus insulting to the host, who will think you suspect him of giving you inferior utensils.
- Don't cross your chopsticks when you put them down. Put them close together, preferably touching, in parallel, below your plate, right in front of your chest.
- Don't put your chopsticks in the communal dishes (the other diners don't want your mouth germs); you may, however, dip into the common wealth with the blunt, holding ends (your companions are not so concerned about what they might catch from your hands, no doubt because they saw you wash them fully on the *oshibori* [hand towel] when you sat down).
- Anything that looks like it should normally be eaten with a spoon should be supped from the bowl. If your soup contains large pieces of food, eat them with your chopsticks and then drink the liquid.

---

hand over your mouth, pop it into your palm, and then lose it in the bowl which should have been provided.

Oranges

Peel an orange with the fingers, break it into segments with the fingers, remove any seeds with the fingers and then eat it with the fingers. Using a knife or a fork at any stage of the operation will make you look as if you are suffering from hyperesthesia.

Oysters

Squeeze the lemon and sprinkle the red pepper over them, then eat the contents with a fork. Then, if it's not a very formal occasion, you may pick up the shell and drink the juice that is left behind. Traditionally oysters were eaten only when there was an R in the month, but since refrigeration techniques have made most foods available year-round, if they're there, tuck in, and certainly don't say, "But it's June."

Peaches

Do I dare to eat a peach? The question troubled T. S. Eliot, but it need not detain us. Cut it into segments, then eat it with the fingers if hard or a fork if ripe.

Pears

Eat a pear in the same way as an apple, using a knife to cut it into quarters and remove the core and the seeds. You may, if you wish, remove the skin, but this is a messy undertaking if the fruit is ripe and it is, in the view of many, something of an affront to the food—a bit like pushing lean pork to the side of the plate and eating only the fat.

Peas

Peas should be eaten from the back of the fork, after having first been pressed onto it by the knife. Although almost everyone I know sometimes eats them using a fork in the same way as they would use a spoon, to do so in "polite company" invites adverse criticism and is therefore giving hostages to fortune.

Pits

At dinner parties, pits and stones should be spat discreetly into a hand held close up against the lips, then placed on the plate. In the absence of plates, use any available ashtray.

Prawns

Peel them manually, wash your fingers in the bowl provided, then use a fork to dip the prawns into the sauce on the side of your plate.

Snails

Unless tongs are provided, it is quite acceptable to hold the shell between the forefinger and thumb while excavating the contents with a fork.

Spaghetti

Hard to eat graciously or delicately, so probably best not served at anything other than the most casual dinner. In Italian theory it should be eaten with the fork alone (using a spoon is not stylish), but in American practice the key objectives are to make as little mess as possible and to avoid sucking it up from the plate.

Sushi

Sushi may be eaten with chopsticks or fingers. Ask for conventional Western cutlery if you must, but expect condescension if you do. If you must use soy sauce, dip—don't saturate. And don't ever put your rice side into the soy sauce; the rice disintegrates on contact and, more importantly, it's not done in proper Japanese etiquette.

Whole Fish

The way you eat a whole fish depends on the type of fish. For *trout*, eat the top part of the body, then remove the head as well as the spine before moving onto the lower half.

The top of *whole sole* should be eaten first, then the spine removed for the bottom filet. *Whitebait* can be eaten whole—heads, tails, bones and all.

DUNKING

Is there a person alive who hasn't dunked his cookie in his tea or coffee? Probably not. Should you do it in polite company? Probably not. Does it "matter" in etiquette terms if you do? I revert to the previous answer. However, those who wish to create a favorable impression would do well to be mindful of the danger that a cookie so immersed may disintegrate 'twixt cup and lip. There are few certainties in human life, but one is that the contract is never awarded to the executive with the sodden shortbread down his front.

FADS AND ALLERGIES

If there is something you cannot or will not eat, you should advise your host in advance, preferably when you accept the invitation. Vegetarians and vegans should not make disapproving remarks about what neighboring carnivores are eating. And vice versa.

FINGER BOWLS

Finger bowls are pretentious unless they are brought to the table with mussels, asparagus or artichokes (in which cases they are essential) or some kinds of fruit. Dip your fingers and wipe them on your napkin, and remember that it's a gesture, not a rite of purification. The water should be tepid. The hostess should avoid putting anything in it—slices of lemon or flower petals, for example—unless she wants her home to be compared with or mistaken for the local tandoori house.

LEAVING THE TABLE

If you need to leave the table during the meal, don't ask like a child and wait for an answer; just say "Please excuse me for a moment" and go off to do whatever it is that you need to do. But don't do it unless it's desperate.

LEAVING YOUR FOOD

The Victorians thought it wrong to eat the last mouthful of anything. Diners were expected to leave a bit of everything in polite little piles around their plates. No one has satisfactorily explained why. Nowadays, things are different. English chef John Burton-Race scrutinizes every plate on its return to his kitchen. "There's nothing more gratifying," he says, "than plates sent back spotless. It's the biggest pat on the back." Burton-Race says he also approves of the French custom of mopping up the plate with bread.

MENUS

A good menu will be varied, and each course should be a counterpoint to that which preceded it. A three-course meal should be complementary. If the *hors d'oeuvre* is heavy, make the main course light. If you serve soup, do not follow it with a casserole, because they are both liquid. Patties should not be followed by pie. If apple sauce is served with the main course, do not serve apple pie for dessert. Melon

THE ORDER OF COURSES
SHOULD BE AS FOLLOWS:

Seafood

Soup or pâté

Sorbet

Fish

Meat or fish plus vegetables or salad

Green salad

Dessert or cheese

Savory

Cheese or dessert

Fresh fruit and/or nuts

Coffee and chocolates and/or liqueurs

and fruit salad should not appear on the same menu. Cheese soufflé should not be followed by cheese. Always serve one hot dish, even on a hot day.

❦

NAPKINS

As soon as you sit down at the table, the napkin on the place setting in front of you should be shaken out of whatever shape it has been folded into and placed on your lap. It is generally regarded as bad manners to anchor it to any part of your clothing or to your person. Do not, for example, tuck it into the front of your shirt collar or your belt.

At the end of the meal, leave the napkin rumpled on the table. To fold it may be taken as an insult because it suggests you think it might be used again before it is washed.

Doilies

These small ornamented napkins often laid on or under dishes are today generally regarded as the epitome of bad taste. Avoid using them and, perhaps, even the people who do.

PLACE CARDS

Place cards at the dinner table should be brief, listing only the person's full name proceeded by their title: Mr., Mrs., Miss or Ms. Do the same for children as they will get a kick out of it.

PORT, *passing the*

The host pours it for the person on his right, then serves himself and passes the bottle or decanter to the left. It then circulates around the table clockwise, and its steady progress should not be impeded—in other words, don't hog it, and don't think that, just because you don't want any, you have no need to involve yourself in its circulation. Port is best served with cheese; some people insist that you can't have one without the other, but this is needlessly pedantic. Port should not be decanted at the table.

SALT

If you want salt and there is on the table a bowl of it with a small spoon, pour a little onto the side of your dinner plate and then distribute it with your knife. If the condiment is in a shaker, feel free to sprinkle it over your food. You may, however, wish to bear in mind that some cooks are embarrassed or even insulted by the implication that they did not use enough seasoning in the preparation. Then again, since many people are now concerned about salt as a cause of high blood pressure, the chef may take the view that he'll cook without and let them add it if they want.

~

SETTING THE TABLE

Glasses

The table is set with a minimum of two wine glasses, one for white and one for red; there may also be a smaller third glass if port and liqueurs are to be served at the end. There is in addition nowadays usually another, larger glass for water.

If you are intending to serve more than one wine of either color, you could put out a different glass for each vintage, so that the one will not infect the other. But that's more trouble than it's worth: Better to stick to a single wine than to make the table look like the Crystal Palace.

Place Settings

Place settings are normally arranged as shown in the diagram on page 68. Note the position of the glasses above the knife tips. The larger glass is for red wine, the smaller for white. A third glass may also be put out if liqueurs are to be served. The outermost knives and forks should be used first; diners should then work their way inward. Dessert implements are shown above the plate, but they can alternatively

be laid beside it. In this case, they should be placed inside the knives and forks nearest to the plates because they will be used last. Standard dinner service knives should be adequate for cutting any meat that is fit to serve—knives with serrated edges are for restaurants. There is nothing to prevent the host from bringing in more cutlery with each course as it is needed, although it may prove noisy and inconvenient to do so.

Serving

You may put bowls of food on the table and get the guests to serve themselves, bring the plates fully loaded to the table, or present the food in some way in between (for example, give them the meat on the plate and let them add their own vegetables).

When serving, you should stand on the guest's left-hand side. Serve the most important female guest first, and the hostess and host last, but otherwise move clockwise around the table. Guests should not start eating before the hostess unless she says "Do start." (Nevertheless, it is better for the hostess to start than to say "Start," because the imperative has matronly or schoolmarmish overtones.) Guests should wait for her cue, no matter how hungry they may be and however much they fear that the food may congeal during the intervening period. The rationale is that there may be a grace. Unless there are servants, it is normally the host who serves the wine and carves the meat. Never clear the table before everyone has finished eating—where do you think you are, a bad restaurant? Coffee can be poured by either the host or the hostess.

~

SOUP

When eating soup, the last drops should be spooned up by tipping the bowl away from you. Soup should be sipped silently from the side of the spoon—putting the whole spoon into the mouth is generally frowned upon.

MORE, OLIVER?

They do say that guests should not ask for seconds of soup. The tortuous rationale is that such a request might be taken to imply that the diners are trying to fill themselves up with what they already know to be palatable through trepidation at what might be in store. But why can't a request for a further helping be taken as a compliment to the chef? Make of it all what you will. Style gurus seem not to object to the idea of the host offering more soup, so presumably in that case it's all right for the guest to accept.

However, if you happen to like putting the whole spoon in your mouth, or find it more comfortable to do so, you can cover any embarrassment felt or caused by telling people that you are from Austria, where the practice is apparently regarded as okay. Don't break bread into your soup. Soup may be served in small cups and drunk like tea.

~

STACKING PLATES

You should not stack plates on or in the immediate vicinity of the dining table, but take them out two by two and stack offstage. Yet many hostesses do stack in plain view, and it doesn't matter very much, even to the sensitive. It is also acceptable to collect plates by holding one in the right hand, balancing another on the forearm, and then stacking in two adjacent piles. Although that is more widely practiced by waitresses than society hostesses, it is, if you can pull it off, impressive in its dexterity. The helpful guest should take his lead from the hostess—if she stacks, you stack; if she doesn't, don't.

Offers of help with the clearing up, though courteous, are seldom welcome, so are probably better not made. The host wants you there for your social warmth and sparkling repartee, not for your skill as a stacker of the dishwasher.

~

SUGAR

In a perfectly polite world, white sugar should be served with tea and coffee. Do not serve sugar cubes unless your home aspires to the condition of ye olde tea shoppe or you are entertaining horses. It is no longer considered necessary to present sugar with tart fruits such as grapefruit.

SUPPER

Supper is the meal eaten after attendance at the theater. Any other meal between sunset and sunrise is dinner. In much of the Midwest, however, "dinner" refers to the noon meal while "supper" is the evening meal.

TABLE MANNERS

Do not put your elbows on the table until the food has been cleared, and preferably not then, either. This rule probably first arose to discourage people from eating sloppily, but it is now just a rule to prevent people from getting comfortable at the table. Also:

DON'T READ AT THE TABLE.

DON'T RISE UNTIL EVERYONE HAS FINISHED EATING.

DON'T LEAN BACK IN SUCH A WAY THAT THE FRONT LEGS OF YOUR CHAIR RISE FROM THE FLOOR.

TEA

Some people are against tea in general, because it is a stimulant and a diuretic and stains the lining of the stomach.

Others would have you believe that tea bags are barbaric, but loose tea is now seldom seen outside huge stainless steel urns in cafés, and most of them now use bags too.

Black tea should be accompanied by a small dish containing very thinly sliced lemon. Each cup should have a saucer and a spoon. When tea is served in the afternoon or in mid-morning ("elevenses"), a small plate should be placed under each cup, which the guest should then remove when cakes or cookies are offered. All other dishes and implements are over the top—there is no need for slop bowls or sugar tongs.

Those who insist on herbal tea appear not to mind their drinks being served to them with the tea bag still in place. But as a host, I wouldn't do it.

MIF

If tea is served, it is widely regarded as classy and impressive to offer a choice of Chinese and Indian. If milk is to be taken, it is conventional to put it in before the tea. This is commonly abbreviated to "MIF" (Milk In First).

The practice originated in the 18th century when tea (then sometimes pronounced "tay") was drunk from china cups that were liable to crack if boiling water was poured straight onto them. Although bone china is now seldom used, there is still a good reason for observing the MIF rule: if the tea starts off weak, you can identify its shortcoming straight away, and pour half cups all the way round, returning to the first guest who will get a strong second half to compensate for the puny beginning. If you put the milk in last, you won't know how weak the brew is until it's too late.

DRINK

Wine

Pairing

This is an area in which it is almost impossible to make any general statement. Among the most common rules are those which state that white wine should be served with white meat and fish, and red wine should accompany dark meat. This will usually save an ignoramus from embarrassment, but it is restrictive and holds good only up to a point. Some of the most striking exceptions are grilled scallops, which may be served with red wine that is light and fresh enough not to overwhelm the flavor of the shellfish; and salted cod, for which a solid red Rioja is more than suitable. The list of possibilities is almost endless, but some of the most common pairings are given on page 74.

One oft-observed rule is that champagne and rosé go with anything. This is not a universal truth but it's reliable often enough if you're desperate. While it is important that the wine should complement the food and neither overwhelm nor be inhibited by it, it is at least as important to ensure that, if more than one wine is served with the meal, none should suffer by comparison with that which preceded it, nor should it overwhelm the grape that follows. Complex foods need simple wines, and vice versa.

When serving wine to guests, don't offer them a choice of drink to accompany their dinner before they know what they're going to eat. You know what they're having, so just bring it on.

RECOMMENDED WINE/FOOD PAIRINGS

Smoked salmon	*Champagne, sparkling wine, Riesling, Sauvignon Blanc*
Grilled fish	*Sauvignon Blanc, Pinot Blanc, Loire Valley whites, Riesling, Champagne*
Pork	*Pinot Noir, red Burgundy, Chianti,*
Lamb	*Cabernet, Merlot, red Bordeaux, Barolo, Rioja*
Roast chicken	*Pinot Noir, red Burgundy, Chianti, Spanish reds*
Steak	*Cabernet, Merlot, red Bordeaux, red Rhones*
Salads	*Sauvignon Blanc, Loire Valley whites*

Serving

Before serving, decant fine red wines and port to separate the liquid from any sediment. Decant port at any time on the day of the dinner, red wine between half an hour and two hours before the guests arrive. Pour it out slowly in a good light so that you can see the dregs at the bottom and prevent them from entering the decanter.

If you're a wine snob, or out to impress, you may wish to decant at the table, thus showing off the labels on your finest vintages. In general, however, it is best not to decant at the table because it requires attention, at least some of which should be devoted to the guests.

Beer

While wine is the generally accepted accompaniment to food, if you have the confidence to bend the rules there is no reason why you should not serve beer as an alternative to accompany a "proper" meal. Some brews are certainly good enough to hold their frothy heads up in the company of almost any cuisine—Red Hook Blonde, for example, goes well with the delicate taste of smoked salmon. Nevertheless, you need either expertise or the hide of a rhino to bring this off, and some people might take it amiss if they are offered only hops and no grapes.

Non-Alcoholic Drinks

Soft drinks, typically still and sparkling water, and possibly orange juice, should always be available. This onus is invariably on the host; it would be odd if a guest turned up bearing a bottle of Evian. You may decide not to serve any alcohol at all. Some guests—particularly those who will have to drive home afterward—may secretly welcome its absence. Never offer one for the road, nor knowingly mix drinks that seem innocuous but are alcoholic. Apart from that, you are dealing with rational adults who should know when they're too drunk to drive home.

IN THE WORKPLACE

No one in his right mind would work were it not for the money. Anyone who claims to do it out of interest or to keep his mind alert is deluding himself. Unless you have the power to change everything that's wrong about your work, pay and conditions, you will have to keep your own counsel; the only incentive is the fear that, if you don't, you may be "released into the job market." Once you reconcile yourself to the indignity of labor, work is little different from other forms of social intercourse. You may wish to appear a go-getter, but getting on with your colleagues is not a sign of weakness.

APPEARANCE

If you turn up to work unshaven or with dishevelled hair or with clothing that makes you look as if you spent the previous night in a doorway, your employers may conclude that if you take no care of yourself you will be insufficiently attentive to your job responsibilities. Although there is a flaw in this reasoning—the slob may be such a perfectionist in his work that he has neither time nor thought for grooming—you should bear in mind that in offices dumb ideas may be more highly valued than truth. Take it from Georges-Louis Leclerc de Buffon, even if you don't believe him, "The style makes the man."

BUSINESS CARDS

The moment for presenting a business card should be chosen with care. It is a well-established national stereotype that Japanese executives give you a card every time they see you, even if they see you eighteen times during the course of a trade fair. Although there are times when you will need to present your card to a flunky before you can get to the person you want to see, the card is usually best presented as you take your leave. It is perhaps presumptuous to flash it at the start of the meeting—the recipient may not like the implication that he might have to deal with you again. On the other hand, if he asks for it, be quick on the draw.

Titles

Since your business card says something about you—
something more than just your name and that of your
company—you should take care over the exact words that
appear on it—especially that of your job title. "Sales
Representative" is fine, but "Area Sales Executive" is
grandiloquent and thus an error of taste.

A card that describes someone as something he is not
is disgraceful. So if you must describe yourself as something,
keep the description close to the truth. Do not use courtesy titles; never, for example, call yourself "Mr.," "Miss,"
"Mrs." or "Ms."

Should you put the letters to which you are entitled
after your name on your card or anywhere else? A small
part of me thinks that if you have earned them, you are
entitled to flaunt them. The greater part, however, takes the
view that if you have a major honor or a degree from an
ancient university, your distinction will shine through
without the need for show. By the same token, no one will
be impressed by a load of letters that mean nothing, and not
even the most cogent explanation will raise his level of awe.

Size

In 1962, Barbara Cartland's *Etiquette Handbook* required a
business or calling card to be "three inches long and one-
and-a-half inches deep." Today, almost anything goes,
although anyone who has tried to keep a contact list of
other people's business cards would prefer it if they were all
still, if not these exact dimensions, at least a consistent size.

COFFEE BREAKS

If you're making tea or coffee, don't just serve yourself, but offer to make a round for nearby colleagues. That goes regardless of whether you are a newly recruited mail-boy or the kind of executive who is taken from meeting to meeting by helicopter. Although there may be difficulties in large open-floor offices with too many people to cater for, your coworkers will probably decline politely but appreciate your courtesy in asking. On the other hand, if you are inundated with affirmative responses, keep an eye on which of the recipients of your generosity reciprocate, and amend your circulation list accordingly.

HIERARCHY

As we have seen, it's seldom the words themselves that cause offense; it's who says them, and when and how. If you see a coworker leaving the office at four o'clock, you can probably get a smile by saying, "Half day?" But if a manager makes the same crack to a filing clerk, it will sound like the kind of shot across the bows that precedes the formal warning.

In the workplace, if you want to talk to a colleague face to face, go to his desk or office. Do not call him in to see you unless you are trying to make a point about your higher place in the corporate pecking order.

~

JOB APPLICATIONS

Job applications are a crucial part of etiquette. They are advertisements for the self, and as with all advertisements the reader is just looking for an excuse to stop reading. So keep them short, direct and professional.

Curriculum Vitae Rules

1) Don't make any spelling mistakes.
2) Don't have a stereotyped CV, which you bang out to anyone and everyone you think might like to give you a job. For each position you choose to pursue, tailor it to bring out particular qualities that may be appropriate for employer A but not for employer B.
3) It is up to you whether you reveal your marital status, your religion and/or your ethnic origins. You may benefit from equal opportunities or positive discrimination, but then again you might not. Remember that these matters are none of anyone else's business.
4) Don't include any education before high school.
5) Don't leave blank years—almost anyone will take such a time gap to mean that you have been in prison.

Asking for References

Referees should be asked in advance. Some prospective employers contact them before replying to you, so beware. They shouldn't, because they might drop you in the shit with your present bosses, but they might.

If someone asks you for a reference, the only polite response is "I'd be delighted." Refusal will signal the end of the relationship.

Do not ask anyone to write a reference for you unless you are convinced that he or she knows your qualities and can be relied upon to give you a good write-up. It is often helpful if the referee is a pillar of the community. Justices of the peace and doctors impress potential employers more than real estate agents and car dealers, even if you're applying for jobs in property or garage management.

Writing References

When it comes to composing a reference, the main rule is: if you can't say anything good, make sure that whatever you do say is couched in terms that will not cause offense. Employers are sometimes bright enough to read between the lines of a testimonial, and omissions can be very informative. And most importantly, don't lie. If you describe as "honest" someone you suspect of having had his hand in your till and he steals in his next job, which he got partly on your recommendation, you can be in trouble with the law. Just say what you can.

~

JOB INTERVIEWS

These disgracefully contrived situations maintain the façade of civilization, but are conducted in the most savage and bloodstained glades of the office jungle. Even though he has just been lowered into a pit full of famished cobras, the interviewee has to be polite and punctiliously observe every one of the important niceties in this book and a couple of thousand unimportant ones besides.

Interviewers, on the other hand, can bare their fangs from the start. Even if they are not overtly hostile, they are likely to form judgments on very little evidence. Thus if the candidate is obese, they are likely to conclude that if he can't control his weight, he will not be able to control his budgets. If he does not dress well, they will presume that he has low self-esteem. This is ridiculous, but it is the way all but the most intelligent and conscientious people think. To make matters worse, throughout the western world, employment is a buyer's market. Companies have no incentive to take special care because there are often thousands more applicants from which to choose.

Most of the "don'ts" for an interviewee are the same as those that apply in polite society. Among other important things to remember are:

1) Never criticize your current employer. You'd probably be well advised not to insult any of the previous ones, either.

2) Some statistical surveys have suggested that the quieter the candidate, the more likely he is to get the job. Well, yes, maybe, but it would be easy to take this to an absurd extreme, and since what one potential employer regards as dignified reticence may be looked upon by another as truculent silence, such studies are of next to no practical value.

3) It is always possible to respond to impertinent personal questions by taking the offensive and replying along the lines of "That's for me to know and you to find out." Nonetheless, wiseacre responses may cause offense and are therefore a violation of etiquette. They are also likely to ensure that you don't get offered the post, which is, after all, the object of the exercise.

ENOUGH EXPERIENCE

While it's probably essential at the interview to talk about your professional experience, once you're there don't go on about your previous jobs. Even if you have been plucked by a head-hunter from the biggest name in the industry, that does not mean that all its practices need to be implemented at your new job. With companies as with other forms of suffering there is no hierarchy: one is as bad as another. Their good points, if any, may be described, but we should learn not to tell our new colleagues at Microsoft that they ordered things better at Apple.

---

4) As much as possible turn minuses into pluses. Don't say "I'm afraid I'm married," but do say, "My wife also has an interest in your micrometer screw gauges."

5) You may reasonably feel that you don't need to answer tomfool questions, but it's important to maintain the veneer of unruffled cooperation. Play them all with a dead bat. The answer to "How do you respond to pressure?" should not be "My eyes tend to roll uncontrollably, I feel nauseous and sometimes I pass out"; the answer to "Do you enjoy working as part of a team?" should not be "No, I'm a sociopath."

∾

NEW RECRUITS

Make newcomers feel at home; help them to get their bearings and to come to grips with the systems that characterize any company. Introduce them to their coworkers and managers.

WORDS OF ADVICE

For Bosses

Your employees are all prostitutes: they only want your money. So don't congratulate them; either put up or shut up. A vote of thanks is, with male nipples, one of the three most useless things in the world.

For Underlings

Don't expect praise. It is only at school that work of a high standard is rewarded the following year by another, more challenging remit. If no one's moaning, you're doing fine.

If you are a senior executive, do not tell new managers as soon as they take up their posts that they are expected to sack some timeserver of whom you happen to have tired or whom you now think you are paying too much. Leave them to make their own judgments. Any manager who does not refuse to comply with such a directive is a worm and should never have been hired.

OFFICE ROMANCE

In most jobs you will be safe for as long as your keep your hands out of the till and off other members of staff. But from time to time colleagues become couples. Any consequent increase in discontent among other members of staff may be attributed to their prudishness or jealousy, but the real cause of bad feeling in such cases is often political—the fear that a new amatory alliance may lead to changes in the *status quo*.

In such instances firms have been known to dispense with the services of one of the lovers; either that or the senior management has made it known that it would like one of them to go. Which is quite wrong, of course. Nevertheless, it might be a good idea for the new couple to keep the relationship as quiet as possible, and for at least one of them to start looking elsewhere.

⌘

RESIGNATION

No matter how strong the temptation to tell your employer where to stick his job, resist it by any means at your disposal, even, as a last resort by reciting this platitudinous workplace mantra:

"On the way up avoid causing pain

To those you may meet on the way down again."

It's a cliché because it's true—remember that you may one day need a reference from them.

Present your resignation in writing and address it to your immediate superior or head of department—don't go over anyone's head. Use words to the effect of: "After ten happy years I write to tender my resignation." (It is probably as well to avoid using the word "offer," you don't want it refused now, do you?) No matter what you really think of the bastard and his chain gang, try if you can to say something like, "I have enjoyed working as part of your team and will be sad to go." It is courteous to say where you're going to work next, but you don't have to.

POST-IT NOT

A friend of mine once left a Post-it note on the computer screen of, as he thought, a male colleague. He had written the message "Call Accounts You Slut." Imagine his surprise when he later returned to the scene to discover that the intended recipient had changed desks, and that his place had been taken by a woman of twenty, who was weeping like Niobe. The moral is that if you can't say something to anyone, you should say it to no one.

SEXUAL HARASSMENT

It's a place of toil, not a wet T-shirt competition in Cancún. Don't say or do anything that will make your colleagues afraid to walk past your desk or accompany you in the elevator. No matter how much you admire their pendulous breasts or their rippling six-packs, keep your aesthetic judgments to yourself.

LANGUAGE
MATTERS

Even the most unambiguous statements have more than one meaning. If you merely tell someone the time, you are imparting additional information about, or creating an impression of, yourself through your accent, tone of voice and choice of words. What goes for speech is also true of written communication. Two people may use the same language to an identical level of proficiency and yet remain mutually incomprehensible because they misunderstand each other's subtexts and nuances. We spend a significant amount of our waking lives trying to avoid the pitfalls of speech — if we remember more of our failures than our successes, that may be because the former are more numerous.

The link between correct use of language and good behavior is complex but strong. The abuse of a term may be every bit as bad as a term of abuse, and every bit as much a violation of etiquette.

AMERICAN ENGLISH AND BRITISH ENGLISH

Oscar Wilde wrote that "We [the British] have really everything in common with America nowadays, except, of course, language." Although some words have sufficiently different meanings to be potential causes of embarrassment, transatlantic cross-fertilization is so great that there is almost never any serious difficulty The minor misunderstandings that occur from time to time arouse mirth rather than irritation. Thus an Englishman in the United States will not cause an international incident when he asks to borrow a rubber: his real meaning will probably be understood, if only from the context, that he wants an eraser and

---

THE QUEEN'S ENGLISH
ACROSS THE POND

My visits to New York have from time to time been troubled by communication breakdowns. A Manhattan bartender once acted as if he didn't understand what I meant when I asked for a "whisky and ice," and only got pouring when I translated the order into a "scotch on the rocks."

On another occasion I went into a newspaper kiosk and asked the vendor if he had any English newspapers. He looked like it was the maddest thing he'd ever heard, and slapped his hand on the *New York Times*, the *Washington Post* and the *Herald Tribune*, with each blow saying "That's English; that's English; that's English." When I told him I meant papers from London, England, he said: "Oh, you mean British newspapers. We don't got no British newspapers."

---

not what some Americans call a prophylactic. Americans hearing a Brit say that Professor Smith enjoyed a fag now and then at Eton will understand that he means a cigarette and not a homosexual, even though the inner workings of the British school system remain impenetrable to anyone without first-hand experience of them.

~

EXPRESSIONS

Never preface anything with "I have to say," because you don't. Let your watchword be the legend on the tablet held by Salvator Rosa (1615–1673) in his self-portrait, *Aut tace aut loquere meliora silentio* (Either keep quiet or say something better than silence).

The following expressions should not be used because they are nauseating to the listener and create the impression that the speaker does not give a fig for sensitive language use:

I kid you not
Believe you me
In my judgment
At the end of the day
I'll tell you for why
I'm not being funny
Period (as in "I'm just not doing that, period.")
A whole different ball game
A touch of the old…
With [all due] respect
To tell you the truth
Quite honestly
To all intents and purposes
This will amuse you
No way, José

TRANSATLANTIC ENGLISH

Some words are problematic because they have different meanings in American English and British English. They include:

Word	American meaning	British meaning
bonnet	baby's hat	front of car
bum	tramp, hobo	buttocks
chips	potato crisps	fried potatoes
comforter	bed quilt	one who comforts
cot	camp bed	infant's bed with high sides
fag	male homosexual	cigarette
fanny	backside	female pudenda
faucet	water tap	pipe inserted into barrel to draw liquid
fender	car bumper	fireguard that hold in the ashes
hood	front of car	covering for the head and back of the neck
pacifier	rubber nipple for a baby to chew on	one who pacifies (almost never used)
pants	trousers	female underwear
pavement	roadway	sidewalk
pecker	the membrum virile	one who pecks
public school	state school	private school
purse	large handbag	small bag for carrying money
rubber	prophylactic	pencil eraser
trunk	car's luggage compartment	elephant's proboscis or luggage

Never begin a speech (or for that matter, any utterance) with "Listen up." It's the "up" that's offensive, partly because it's ungrammatical, but mainly because it has the effect of turning into an instruction what should rightly only be a request.

Disreputable Argument

In conversation, avoid saying anything that leaves no room for contradiction. So don't say "You can't tell me anything I don't know about that: I've been a teacher/brain surgeon/actress/publisher/professional jockey for thirty years."

The fact that you did a thesis on Shelley neither trumps nor invalidates the views held by a recreational reader of the poet's oeuvre; you may have treated more sublimated Oedipal complexes than I have had hot dinners, but that does not necessarily rule out my explanation of the boy's relationship with his mother. Of course it may be that your superior knowledge has given you greater insight, but you have to prove it in the stern heat of light conversation. Don't wave your diplomas around like offensive weapons: they qualify but they do not entitle.

MEANINGS

Those who do not know the difference between "refute" and "deny," and "flaunt" and "flout" (90 percent of journalists and politicians) may cause offense to those who do, and should therefore try harder to get it right.

- You can be said to refute a charge only if you prove it to be untrue. Thus a counter-assertion is not a refutation, as is popularly supposed, it is merely a denial.

- The girls may flout the school rules by wearing crop-tops, but in doing so they flaunt their suntans.

Other Misused Terms

"**Hopefully**" should be rendered in English as "it is to be hoped that." Thus the famous dictum "To travel hopefully is a better thing than to arrive" would come to mean "it is to be hoped that to travel is better than arriving." Which, it need hardly be added, was not what Robert Louis Stevenson meant when he wrote it.

"**Chauvinist**" is not the right word to describe men who treat women badly and who disapprove of them having equal opportunities. "Male chauvinist" is no better. The word "chauvinism" is derived from Nicolas Chauvin, a veteran of the Napoleonic wars, and means only absurd pride in one's country, with a corresponding contempt for other nations. The term that should be used is "sexism."

Natives of and things originating in the South American country known as "**Argentina**" are "Argentines" or "Argentine." "Argentinian" means someone from Argentinia, and there is no such place.

A "**parameter**" is a mathematical term, which does not mean the same—or anything like the same—as "perimeter," "boundary" or "limit," as it is currently popular to believe.

"**Pristine**" means "restored to its former state," not "in mint condition."

An **enormity** is a great crime, it is not "anything that is difficult."

It is redundant to describe a period or a time as a **period of time**, except in an unlikely context where it may be confused with menstruation or a punctuation mark. Convicts do not do periods of time.

The germs of other illiteracies are still alive and contagious. A commentator is one who comments: there is no such verb as "**to commentate**." Almost everyone gets this wrong.

Between you and I is illiterate, and its use is offensive to all those who know better.

There are no degrees of **uniqueness**. A person or thing is either unique or not unique: "very unique" is always wrong. ("Almost unique," on the other hand, is okay.)

Gay

The appropriation of the blameless, non-sexual word "gay" to mean "homosexual" is regrettable, but not as bad as the subsequent division of homosexuals into "gays" (male homosexuals) and "lesbians" (female homosexuals). The only possible reason for this absurdity is that people are under the impression that the "homo" in "homosexual" derives from the Latin *homo*, meaning "man." Well it doesn't, it comes from the Greek *homos*, meaning "same." So "homosexual" covers both male and female homosexuals. Nevertheless, the kindly will note that anyone who uses the old word today may be taken for a homophobe rather than a lover of language.

Gender

There is always someone who will write "Yes please" in the space on the form next to "Sex." But "sex" definitely requires the answer male or female. "Gender" is correctly a grammatical term: nouns and pronouns have masculine, feminine, neuter or common genders.

Nowadays, however, "gender" is frequently used instead of "sex." The supposed grounds for this are that people only appear to be male or female, and they might perceive themselves as something other.

Lavatory

Fowler's *Modern English Usage* deprecates the euphemistic use of the word "lavatory." Today, gentlemen will call this room the bathroom, the most accurate of the polite terms in use. But for most people, anything goes. Some of the options are polite, others are uncouth. Other possibilities include:

- the men's room or ladies' room
- the toilet
- the restroom

Iconoclasts and hellraisers may dare to call it:

- the crapper
- the pisser
- the shithouse

How these go over depends both on the élan with which they are delivered and the tastes of the audience.

Partner

A partner is a business associate. Unfortunately, the term has been stretched by those who are too old or too inhibited, to describe their amatory or sexual companions as "lovers," "boyfriends" or "girlfriends."

If you introduce someone of the same sex as your partner, it may be unclear whether you mean business- or life-partner. It is to be hoped that your new acquaintance will not be so crass as to ask directly: "Are you gay?"; nevertheless, the question will hang in the air, and thus cause embarrassment until it is answered. The problem is not relieved by gay marriage: couples do not generally describe themselves as "husband" and "wife," for several reasons, all of which are good. Gay couples just say, "We're married."

PLURALS

The use of the wrong plural will not cause offense, but it may embarrass those who know better because they will worry that if they then use the correct term themselves in the illiterate's hearing he may feel that he is being condescended to.

"**Economics**" and "**politics**" are conventionally singular, although they don't look it.

The plural of "**fish**" can be "**fishes**" but seldom is.

One **goose**, two or more **geese**, but one **mongoose**, two or more **mongooses**.

"**Media**" and "**criteria**" are the plurals of, respectively, "medium" and "criterion."

The plural of "**stadium**" is "stadia," but after all the talk of the new stadiums that will be built in London for the 2012 Olympics I fear I've given up on this, at least until after the closing ceremony.

"**Police**" is strictly singular, but only the most strict grammarian would insist on "The police is investigating."

"**Government**" is trickier: on the basis of usage you could make a case for singular or plural. Choose which you prefer, stick to it, and be confident that neither version will make you seem illiterate as long as it's applied consistently.

POLITICAL CORRECTNESS

Political correctness (PC) strives to avoid implied elitism, colonialism, racism and sexism in the use of language. Thus those who were once known as Red Indians are now to be called "Native Americans" or "First Nation." Previously animate chairmen have undergone a metamorphosis into "chairs"; the physically handicapped are sometimes described as "the differently abled."

This is largely well-intentioned, nonsense codified by bores (the differently interesting). If the United States is not vigilant it may follow Britain, where highway construction sites and other such places have signs bearing the legend "Operatives at Work." You can see that the people who came up with that vile phrase had some relationship with

---

SOCIAL SITUATION

At lunch with a business contact who I thought might help me advance in my career, he happened to mention that he had a son named Linus. "Aha," I said, quickly grasping the opportunity to show expertise and establish a greater rapport, "you named him after Linus Pauling, chemist, double Nobel laureate and champion of vitamin C as a prophylactic against all forms of cancer."

"No," he replied. "We named him after the character in the Peanuts cartoons."

---

the language—they plainly recognized that 'Workers at Work' was a pleonasm—but lacked the confidence to over-rule the silly objection that "Men at Work" may appear to exclude women. Nonsense.

No matter what linguistic egalitarians may groundless-ly assert, it is still perfectly permissible to talk about "Man" when you mean "all men and women (mankind)," and you can still use masculine pronouns as common gender, as in "everyone has his faults." Indeed, you'd be verging on illit-erate not to. But if you insist on maintaining these stan-dards, you must be prepared to justify them and to defend yourself against attacks by people who will describe you as "reactionary" or "unreconstructed." (Sticks and stones....)

Compare:

"To boldly go where no man has gone before."

Star Trek (1964)

"To boldly go where no one has gone before."

Star Trek: The Next Generation (1987)

PRONUNCIATION

"It is impossible for an Englishman to open his mouth without making some other Englishman despise him."

George Bernard Shaw, Preface to *Pygmalion*

The differences between American and British pronuncia-tion are notable and sometimes amusing ("You say to-*may-*

to, I say to-*mah*-to") but no big deal in etiquette terms as long as you don't try to be something you are not. There are few worse things than an obvious American affecting an English accent, and almost no one can carry it off, although Renee Zellweger came close in the film *Bridget Jones' Diary*. And there is no more repellent sound under the sun than that of a Brit trying to do American pronunciation.

Here are some of the words that are pronounced differently on either side of the Atlantic; stick to the way they say them in your native land.

Leisure is *lee-zhur* in America and *le-zhur* in Britain.

Medicine should have three syllables (med-i-sin), not two (med-sin).

Schedule should be *sked-yule* if you're American but *shed-yule* if you speak British English.

Americans stress the second syllable of oregano, Britons the third.

The short first e in "leverage" is long in Britain.

The Brits get the most out of laboratory, which has at least four syllables and may even have five; they regard "labra tree" as cutting corners.

How can so many people pronounce nuclear as if it were spelled "nucular"? You can't blame President George W. Bush for that, although at the time of writing he is the highest-profile offender—it was current before he came to prominence.

Affectation

Still it's better to say all words wrongly than to sound affected. Some of the most prominent Britons have suffered the ill-effects of elocution coaching. Margaret Thatcher and her predecessor as Conservative leader, Edward Heath, both came from lower middle class backgrounds and learned to speak "nobbily" at Oxford University. Or rather half learned, as their vowel sounds always betrayed their origins.

There's nothing wrong with making good—you've just got to make sure that, having done it, you speak naturally in a way that's sometimes described as "staying true to one's roots." Jamie Lee Curtis did so when she married a British lord—she kept speaking like a girl from L.A. should. Madonna, meanwhile, took her marriage to English film director Guy Ritchie as a cue to adopt an accent that was strange by any standards.

Personal Names

Only a fool would use one particular name to represent a type of which he disapproves. If you say "He's a real Kevin," you can bet that will be the name of the father of the person to whom you are speaking.

~

SWEARING

You can now get away with almost anything coarse or scatological in most company, except that of known puritans such as senior members of one's own family. "Fuck," if not yet commonplace, is widespread in the street, in the drawing room and in the broadcast media.

The word that you still cannot say is the so-called "C-word," which is cunt: this remains unacceptable, and is offensive in almost any context, whether spoken or written.

Swear words become civilized much faster than many of those who use them. Yesterday's taboos are sanitized today in preparation to become parts of tomorrow's conventional vocabulary. "Chicano" was a pejorative U.S. term for Mexican Americans until they repossessed it as a badge of pride in their ethnic identity. The "N" word has been embraced by some in the African-American community, although white people should still never use the term.

"Ho" is a jive form of "whore": the latter might be frowned on, but the former is now often jocose.

It's still hard to get away with "motherfucker," but "mofo" is widely used and causes less offense than the full version.

"Bitch" has had its teeth drawn through overuse, and may even be used affectionately.

Despite a general relaxation in attitudes to swearing, many people are still more impressed by a man who is master of polite and noneuphemistic vocabulary than by one who curses like an Italian prostitute.

The problem with foul-mouthed speech today is that it tends to put the swearer in the wrong, or at least to weaken his case. If someone knocks into you and you respond with "Watch where you're [insert expletive of choice] going," your assailant may choose to take offense at your bad language. So through the injudicious use of a single word in the heat of the moment, you have renounced the high moral ground and ended up in what insurance agents call a knock-for-knock situation.

JOKES

In all forms of social intercourse, from chatting at a cocktail party to speech-making on a formal occasion, remember that it is perfectly possible to be amusing without being risqué. This is not a puritanical blast against dirty jokes; it's merely a reminder that there are prudes and puritans everywhere, and it is better not to cause offense. It is advisable always to err on the side of caution.

The most self-assured—or, perhaps, the most careless—can get away with almost anything. This is partly a matter of tone and timing. It is sometimes even possible to get away with dirty jokes and other forms of tastelessness by emphasizing that you are quoting someone else—this isn't my sense of humor, you understand, but I am fascinated by the mentality of those who do regard it as amusing. Chaucer got away with that approach, but it is potentially hostile terrain, to be entered at your own peril.

MEETING
PEOPLE

Meeting presidents, clergy, the famous, the poor, the dull and even the worthless . . . This chapter attempts to show you how to act when you encounter them at social events, while retaining both your virtue and the common touch; it even suggests a few possible topics of conversation that might engage the most taciturn and self-regarding. Try not to be put off by another person's chilliness—remember that once you've broken the ice you can gambol in the cold water underneath.

BOWING

Bowing should be done to royalty only, and even with royalty it is no longer de rigueur. Thus, a cat may look at a king and even the staunchest republican can hold his head up in the Queen's presence without running the risk of having it cut off the following morning. If you do bow, bow with the head only—do not bow from the waist.

In Asia, however, different rules apply, and Americans may obey them when dealing with people from that continent, not least because it would be embarrassing to offer a handshake and receive a bow in return. The Japanese, for example, bow in greeting: the deeper the bow, the greater their veneration for the other person.

INTRODUCTIONS

The polite way to make introductions is to present the "lesser" person to the "greater." The younger should be introduced to the older, the man to the woman, the commoner to the peer of the realm, and the mailboy to the VIP:

"Richard, this is Tommy Tucker;
Tommy, Richard Branson"

or

"Have you met Tommy Tucker?
Richard Branson."

Couples

When introducing couples who are not married to each other, it is usually better not to draw attention to the fact that they are a unit. If their relationship emerges naturally during the course of the conversation, fine, but a good host will avoid implying that anyone is merely someone else's appendage. Indeed, the same courtesy may be extended to married couples: Jane may be delighted to be introduced as "John's wife," but if there is the slightest possibility that she may feel inhibited or demeaned by being thus put into context, make her plain "Jane."

What goes for heterosexual couples applies also to homosexuals: you should never "out" people in a social setting. If they want their orientation to be publicized, they will say so themselves.

Family

If you are introducing your own parents to a newcomer, you should use the names by which you would yourself address them (mom, mother, dad, father or whatever). Thus you leave it to your parents to invite their new acquaintance to call them by their forenames if they so wish. If they do not extend such an invitation, it should be clear to the newcomer that they wish to be addressed by their titles and surnames until further notice. The same rule applies to grandparents; with aunts and uncles, you may use your discretion. Some children introduce their parents this way: "My Dad, Winston," "My Mom, Shania." That's good etiquette as long as it's previously been cleared—tacitly or explicitly—with the fossils themselves.

If you are being introduced to the parents of your friend or lover, address the parents by their titles and surnames unless otherwise directed; allow the parents to correct your formal address if they so desire.

Famous People

Do not gloss the famous person's introduction; do not, for example, say "Richard Branson, Chairman of the Virgin group of companies." A good wine needs no bush. If I were to introduce you to Tenzin Gyatso, neither you nor he would want me to add "aka the Dalai Lama, the exiled spiritual leader of Tibet."

AN EASY ESCAPE ROUTE

Fortify yourself with the thought that the famous are probably every bit as nervous about you as you are about them. When novelist Kingsley Amis met people for the first time, he would sometimes invite them to his club, The Travellers'. He would arrange that during lunch a friend would appear and ask him, "Has the Mozart record arrived?" If the reply was "No," the friend would know that Kingsley was enjoying his new acquaintance and leave them to it. However, if Kingsley was bored he would answer "Yes" and immediately adjourn to go and get it, leaving the unwelcome guest to find his own way off the premises.

Author's note: this sly trick was first made public by Anthony Powell in his Journals 1982–86. I can confirm it from personal experience: when I lunched with Amis a fellow indeed pitched up and asked that self-same question. By then, the writer had been talking to me about himself for some time and appeared annoyed by the interruption. He rather snapped at him, I felt, saying no, it had not arrived. "I think you'll find it has, you know, Sir Kingsley," I protested.

There's no need to endure a dark night agonizing about any of this. All you have to do is make sure that the two parties get to hear each other's names. Once you've done that, you have played your part and can duck out and circulate.

If you are not one of those who can speak on any topic, you will probably feel more at ease if you do not launch straight in on the subject for which the famous person is best known.

Comedian Emo Philips was accosted
by a stranger who asked him rudely:
"Have I seen you on television?" To which he
replied: "I'm afraid I don't know. Unfortunately,
you can't see through the other way."

Girlfriend/Boyfriend

Don't feel that you have to introduce your significant other with an explicit description of his or her role in your life. "This is Caroline; we're an item" can hardly fail to embarrass the audience and make the woman think she's a trophy, a notch on the bedpost, a mere extension of the speaker's ego, or all three. If you do feel like letting your relationship be known, simply say "This is Caroline, my girlfriend," and leave it at that.

"I Remember You"

What do you do if the person to whom you have just been introduced says that of you but you have no recollection of him? This hasn't happened to me often, but when it has, I seldom feel that I've got my response completely right. I tend to squint myopically and say "Aaah, yes, of course" in a way that I imagine comes across as faintly suspicious. So although I do not prescribe that approach, I think it's preferable to a flat contradiction—if he's right, and you've simply forgotten him, or if you're right and he's confusing you with a mass murderer, there will be embarrassment. The best tip is to the person who purports to do the recognizing: say where you previously met, but make sure it wasn't somewhere like a brothel.

Latecomers

When you have to introduce tiresome late arrivals long after all the other guests have been presented to each other, cut corners in order to avoid disrupting the conversation which it is to be hoped will by now be in full flow. Say their names once to the assembly, and then tell them the names of the first couple of people who meet them close up.

Professionals

Do not ask lawyers "How can you defend someone if you know he's guilty?" and do not expect free on-the-spot medical advice from doctors. Both professions would almost rather be asked how much they earn.

Titles

Guests with several titles can be introduced with only their main one, or the one of which they're most proud, or that which explains the capacity in which they're at the event. Thus the ambassador "His Excellency Dr. Sir Henry Wooton" may have some of his titles omitted in the interests of brevity and of not overawing other guests. However, if you know that His Excellency likes to hear them all, or suspect that he might, make sure he gets them.

If you have forgotten the names or titles of your guests yourself, you have a choice. You can either brazen it out by saying "You all know each other," or you can be honest and say "I must apologize, I've had a complete mental blank." The latter takes guts, and it is better not to attempt it unless you are sure you can carry it off. Remember that etiquette is only breached if offense is caused.

PUNCTUALITY

" L'exactitude est la politesse des rois. "

(Punctuality is the politeness of kings.)

Louis XVIII *(attributed)*

Hosts at restaurants should always arrive before their guests. Cocktail and drinks parties do not go on for long, so guests should try to make it within fifteen to thirty minutes of the stated starting time. It is permissible to be up to an hour late for evening parties at which there is no meal; if it's dinner, you should arrive about ten minutes after the time the host has suggested. Children should be taken to and collected from children's parties punctually—plus or minus five minutes at most.

At a routine rendezvous, my rule is this: if I'm not supposed to be insulted if they're ten minutes late arriving, I assume they won't be insulted if I leave after waiting for eleven minutes.

SHAKING HANDS

Most people shake hands with each other when they meet for the first time. Some people shake hands every time they meet, even if they encounter each other every day. Such people are usually—but not always—foreigners. Everyone must decide whether or not he approves of this, and acquiesce or resist as directed by his conscience.

Grasp the proffered hand normally and firmly: do not attempt to make the moment memorable by breaking a couple of its proximal phalanges. Even more important, do not hold the grip and the gaze of the recipient until it causes embarrassment. You don't need to take your glove off for a handshake, but it adds a stylish flourish if you do. Men should always stand to shake hands; women may remain seated even if the other person is standing.

KISSING HELLO

Occasionally you will find yourself in a circle that practices kissing hello. Some confine themselves to one kiss on the cheek; others often insist on both cheeks. If you get it wrong—in other words, if you go for a different number of kisses from that which the other person is expecting to give and receive—you will embarrass yourself.

Almost everyone finds air kissing annoying, but many people do it. So how should we deal with it? We could take the prescriptive approach and point out to offenders the error of their ways. But what would be the point? Do you really want the sensation of their lips against your cheeks so badly that you're prepared to ask them for it? Are you prepared to say that you find their refusal to put their mouths on your body offensive?

Public Puckering

Traditions evolve by which you will kiss some of your acquaintances every time you see them, and leave others unosculated. So what do you do when you meet someone you habitually kiss in the company of someone else you know and do not? There is no easy answer to this, save the advice that you should either kiss all your friends every time you meet them like some drugged-up theatrical novelist, or none of them under any circumstances. The spirit of the age would appear to dictate that those who do not kiss everything that moves are somehow repressed, but others would say that kissing is too good to be wasted by putting on a public performance.

Between the Sexes

This chapter is based on the premise that copulation is not the only thing implied by "sexual intercourse." The term is taken to include all dealings between man and woman that are informed—or more likely inhibited—by the one's consciousness of the other's pudenda. Because most of us spend the whole of our earthly sojourn confined in a single sex, and few of us have the imagination of a Tolstoy, there is plenty of scope for misunderstanding and conflict. Numerous barriers remain between people of different sexes even if they are not, haven't been and will never be a couple.

If you need to be told that it is wrong to thrust yourself upon unwilling parties, or to make pre- and post-game comparisons with previous conquests, you probably need counseling rather than a book of this type.

ADULTERY

"Do not adultery commit;
Advantage rarely comes of it."

A.H. Clough, *The Latest Decalogue*

Adultery is generally frowned upon, although some people like it, and some people have spouses who like them to like it. Unless you are a clergyman or a right-wing politician, it is a mistake to condemn someone's adultery out of hand before you know all the circumstances. It is not done to confess or prate to a third party of one's own infidelity. To do so is even worse than boasting of premarital sexual conquests, and a deal riskier.

AN ALIEN PRACTICE

It is noteworthy that in English, adultery is often regarded as something that foreigners do:

"What men call gallantry, and gods adultery,
Is much more common where the weather's sultry."
—George Gordon Byron, Lord Byron, *The Corsair*

And the nationality that most often takes the rap is the French:

"Fidelity means nothing, but to stand before God
after death and confess you have never cheated
on your wife—what a humiliation!"
—Jules Renard

ASKING SOMEONE OUT

The only consolation that can be offered to young people who suffer from embarrassment is that they will not always feel it. Sooner or later it withers and falls away, as the snake sloughs its skin. But in the meantime asking someone out on a date is one of the most frightening social leaps that a youth can make. The trick is to frame the invitation in such a way that both parties are left with an honorable path of retreat. Tell the invitee that you're going out with a bunch of friends, and ask her if she would care to join you. That way she gets the idea that you are interested, but has neither to say that she finds you the antidote to desire nor to enter a contract for life.

An invitation to dinner à deux may or may not be seen as a sexual overture, it depends on the circumstances. It's okay if the proposed venue is a restaurant—it's a public place and the exits are not barred, so both parties have a means of escape if need be. It may even be okay at home. There is no need to take the mystery out of the underlying purpose, if any, of the date—don't say anything along the lines of "on the understanding that it's purely platonic" or "I want you to know there's more to this than just dinner." Neither party should assume too much. Hope is more fun than certainty, but uncertainty creates fear: the middle way is narrow, but it is not un-navigable.

No One Wants to Hear How Happy You Are

It may be that you want or need to repel someone's advances because you are already taken with or by another. If that's the case, you don't necessarily need to tell the suitor point-blank that you are married or content in a long term sexual relationship; find a way of dropping it into the conversation in a plausible context. And a word to the suitor: take note of the information thus imparted and consider yourself warned off; be grateful that you have suffered no loss of face; don't say "Are you getting enough?"

Some Other Time

This no longer means anything other than "Not in a million years." So if you really can't make the suggested date, but would like to go out with the person who's asking, you must either suggest a specific alternative ("The 19th's out, I'm afraid. What about the 23rd?") or make it clear in another way, perhaps by saying: "I can't make the Mozart, but there's a season of Vivaldi coming up in June that I'd really like to go to. Would you be interested in that?" If that goes over well, either of you can get the tickets: there's no longer any reason why it should only be the man.

BREAKING UP

The point of the break up is to free yourself from a no-longer useful or pleasing attachment. The point is *not* to hurt the other's feelings by letting them know what bottom-feeding troglodytes they are and how they've done nothing but make your life miserable for the past ten months. (If they were so terrible, how come you dated them for so long?) Instead, be as calm and courteous as possible, while still being direct to get your point made, but without hurting the other any more than necessary—this way, you might remain friends or, at the very least, you won't have one more ex out there infecting other potential mates with bilious stories of your vileness.

Of course, this bit of etiquette assumes that you are able to use logic in a very emotional situation. And since when have matters of the heart operated on logic rather than emotion?

DINNER DATES

The romantic dinner may be likened to an aircraft's final approach: both the pilot and the ground controller are expecting a landing, but both remain constantly mindful of the possibility that the plane may reroute at the last moment. There may be a point of no return, but it will never be reached while you remain seated at the table.

Who Pays

The man should offer, but he shouldn't protest too vigorously if the woman insists, either on paying half or on taking the full force of the blow. Her response may be taken as an indication of the passability of the path to the bedroom, but it is not a sure sign, so don't jump to conclusions.

Ordering Food

I was only once in a restaurant that brought my companion a lady's menu, and I assume that the practice is moribund if not already defunct. If it isn't it ought to be, not least because I spent half the evening getting her to guess how much each dish cost.

Some egomaniacs like to take everyone's order and then pass it on to the waiter, thus showing that they have marvelous memories and (more importantly) that they're in charge. More balanced people realize that if their com-

---

SOCIAL SITUATION

A man once told me about a time he had been unfaithful to his wife. This is not in itself an unusual occurrence—people often feel an irresistible need to boast of their conquests. I have wondered why, but never identified a satisfactory explanation—all I can think is that they want to impress the audience. Two particular details made this confidence, which I need hardly add I had not solicited, especially distasteful. The minor one was circumstantial: he gave it a sordid local habitation—a hotel in Brussels while on a business trip. The major one was that he seemed to have forgotten that I knew him only through his poor wife, who had been my friend for 15 years, and who introduced him at a painful "meet my new significant other" evening shortly before they became engaged. Plainly this is a dilemma; how should one resolve it?

I can only tell you what I did not do. I did not warn him that he should not be telling me such a thing, because of course by the time I realized what he was saying he had already said it. I did not look disgusted, and I did not affect awe. I made like the Sphinx. Moreover, I did not tell the betrayed woman. So instead of answering the question, I merely put another: who is demeaned by this? Not the coxcomb who publicized his Belgian swordsmanship; nor yet the wife, who as far as I am aware knows nothing of it to this day. No, the only net loss was sustained by the poor creature who had to hear the confession and then felt obliged to keep it to himself. I wish now that I'd gone the whole hog on the Sphinx front and hurled the ghastly traveler to his death on some nearby rocks.

---

panions were incapable of coherent speech they wouldn't have come out for dinner, so leave them to express their desires for themselves.

Topics for Discussion

Many of us have skeletons in the closet. But the romantic dinner is not the confessional: try to save tales of the abusive stepparent and the ball-breaking ex for another occasion.

THE GALLANT GENTLEMAN

It is no longer expected that every polite man will open doors for women, pull out their chairs for them when they are about to sit down, and help them off and on with their coats. Indeed, some women may regard such gestures as violations of their independence. Others, however, still like to receive such courtesies or at least to appear submissive.

The modern man is therefore faced with a choice: he should either adopt a policy and stick to it (in which case he'd probably do better to leave them be, unless they're clearly struggling) or else judge each case on the available evidence. A man may get away with a perfunctory attempt at assistance; if he meets even the slightest opposition he should not push it, and regard himself as warned.

"I'M PREGNANT."

When your girlfriend or wife utters these two words, the correct response is not "Whose is it?" Nor should you scream in agony and go running for the nearest exit. Even if the pregnancy was unplanned, it is still your responsibility to deal with the consequences. With any luck, each of you will already know where the other stands on abortion, because now is not the time for a philosophical argument about the point at which life begins. Now is the time for comfort and decisive action. Both parties are equal members of this discussion and should not shirk any of their duties. The man should support the woman and, except in exceptional and extreme circumstances that are beyond the purview of this book, the woman should stick around to be supported. If you decide to have the baby, it's time to start painting the guest room in pastel colors and kicking your bad habits.

INTERNET DATING

The principles of regular dating apply quite well here: be yourself, don't lie, etc. The only problem is: the temptation to disavow these principles is much stronger with iDating than with the regular style of dating (you know, the style without the trendy lower case "i" in front of it). With your online profile, it's so easy to create a façade of a better you (funnier, younger, thinner, richer, more clever, less married, etc.). But so what? So you get them interested. Then what? You're going to have to meet people eventually, and then they're bound to be disappointed with the real you. But if you create an accurate profile of yourself, you'll be pre-selecting someone who might actually be compatible with the real you. Honesty works. Go figure.

JEALOUSY

It is an error of taste to display jealousy. If your partner is making advances to someone else in your presence, leave him to make a fool of himself: moral superiority and cool-headedness give you an unbeatable hand. If you assert yourself or lose your temper, you will lose—you are demeaned by engaging in the farce. Never give anyone the satisfaction of knowing he has annoyed you, and remember that if he is going to run away with the person with whom he is cavorting, he'll do it whether you defend your territory or not. Above all, there is no less aesthetically appealing sight in social life than that of two people fighting about fidelity.

PICKING UP WOMEN

Women are under constant barrage from all manner of men trying to seduce them in the sleaziest, least imaginative ways possible. You have to be very careful to separate yourself from these lecherous hordes lest you become one of them in her mind's eye. Straightforward and direct ("Hi, my name's Will.") is therefore better than some cheesy, cringe-inducing come-on ("Do you have a mirror in your pants? Because I can sure see myself in them.").

Along these same lines, do not try too hard to impress a woman. Unless you are an egotist simply looking for an audience, you should be sizing up her, just as she is sizing up you. In any case, why should all the decision making be left to the girls? If she fails to impress you, you should have the pride to move on to a woman more worthy of your affections. Don't go for any port in a storm.

Luckily for you, historical man has set the bar quite low when it comes to seducing women. If you can actually engage your prey in real conversation, you will be far ahead of 99 percent of your competition. And if the thought of actually conversing with a woman you've never met before seems impossible, know that all it takes is to show interest in what she is saying, ask leading questions that further the conversation, and demonstrate some sort of opinion about the matter in question. Voilà: conversation.

∽

THE PROPOSAL

The proposal sets the tone for the rest of the marriage. Are you going to be cute and silly (Ring tied to the collar of your beloved pet. Here Fifi!), or romantic and charming (a starry night on the beach in the Bahamas)? How about adventurous (at the peak of Machu Picchu)? However you choose to propose, make sure it is something special for both of you. Pause and ask yourself "Does *she* want to get engaged on the Jumbotron at Yankee stadium, or do *I*?"

It doesn't matter where you propose, or the exact form of words you use. The man might go down on one knee, but then again if he is proposing to a woman with a strong sense of irony he might be better advised not to. And remember that in the 21st century women can propose to men at any time.

A true gentleman will have thought beyond the big question to have made post-engagement plans. Off to a hotel? Dancing? A bottle of champagne? To mom and dad's to announce the news? The last thing you want for your first moments as an engaged couple is to share an awkward exchange: "So what do you want to do? I don't know, what do you want to do? Umm…."

PUBLIC DISPLAYS OF AFFECTION

The incipient stages of a relationship are generally highly sexually charged. New lovers can rarely keep their hands off one another. But for pity's sake, when you're out in public, show a little self-restraint. A quick kiss hello is fine, as is holding hands. But nobody (except for the most lascivious of peeping Toms) wants to see you two sitting on each other's laps, petting one another, and shoving your tongues into the back of each other's throats.

OLD FLAMES

What if you used to have a secret or long-forgotten liaison with someone who is, was or has since become famous? Should you tell others—your intimates or anyone who will listen—of the big one that got away? Circumstances alter cases, but in general it is better to keep these conquests or submissions quiet. Apart from being ungallant, such talk smacks of desperation, sounding as if you need to prove your (former) desirability or man-of-the-worldliness. Moreover, it is like Graham Greene's claim that he played solitary Russian roulette: impressive if true, but unverifiable.

SEXUALLY TRANSMITTED DISEASES

To avoid sexually transmitted diseases (STDs), manners' guru Moyra Bremner advised people to ask each other just before they go to bed together for the first time if they have any. This idea is as affecting in its simplicity as it is preposterous as a realistic course of action. Does no one lie about these things? Did no one ever forget one or two small inconvenient details about himself when the blood was hot? And if it turns out that one participant has a full house of venereal conditions, to what extent is the other partner indemnified by earlier assurances to the contrary? None whatsoever.

Of course, if you ask the question and get an affirmative answer, or better still, if your prospective lover confesses in advance without prompting, at least you know where you stand. (The problem of precisely when to ask or when to announce the bad news remains tricky—over the coffee

---

ARE YOU NOW OR HAVE YOU EVER BEEN...?

Asking people point-blank or making speculative assertions about their sexual orientation ("I always thought you were gay") may cause offense. And doing so takes out one of the best parts of life: gradual discovery.

---

or between the sheets?) But if you ask the question and you get a no, you will still have to use your judgment.

Both the hunter and the quarry should probably always carry condoms and as many good luck charms as they can decently have about their person without appearing too superstitious. The former accoutrements should, however, be kept under cover. It is presumptuous, and hence an error of taste, to have them on semi-show at the top of an open handbag or sticking out of the back pocket.

~

STANDING

Men who are seated should stand when a woman enters or re-enters the room at a formal or even slightly smart occasion. It is sometimes necessary to use one's judgment over this and avoid bobbing up and down ludicrously as she comes in and out of the room. There is usually no need to do it if there are numerous guests and the female arrival is at the far end of the table. If you are in mid-course, just carry on eating unless it is a particularly formal occasion, in which case a small bob in which the buttocks are lifted a couple of inches from the seat of the chair will suffice; there is no need to go for full elevation.

On trains and buses, seats should be given up only in cases of need. It is no longer the done thing for a man to offer a woman his seat if there are no others available simply because she is a woman. If the woman is pregnant, carrying a small child or in any kind of apparent difficulty, a seat should be offered. It is perfectly in order for a woman to offer her seat to a man, but again this should be done only in case of need and should not be interpreted by the man as a come-on.

WALKING WITH WOMEN

According to medieval tradition, when a man walked with a woman he was supposed to position himself on her right-hand side, so that his sword arm was free and far enough away from her so that he did not bang her with his scabbard. Today, however, few are so armed in public; nevertheless, the custom survives, although it may be preferable for the man to position himself so that he is closer than his female companion to passing road traffic. Again, neither party should make a song and dance about this: the woman should not insist on such treatment, and the man should not draw attention to the fact that he is doing it.

Escalators

Even in an age of women's liberation and equal opportunity, it is still common for the man to go ahead of the woman on an escalator. On a down escalator, this is to ensure, in the event of an emergency stop, that the woman's fall may be cushioned by the man (the male of the species is still usually acknowledged as physically stronger than the female). On an up escalator, it is also to prevent the man looking up the woman's skirt. Do not insist on this custom at all costs, however. The purpose of such a courtesy is to ease the running of society; it is not an end in itself. Your obituary will mention your career, your parents, school, university, wife and children, usually in that order; it will almost certainly pay no tribute to the manner in which you conducted yourself between the second and third floors of Macy's.

Revolving Doors

Revolving doors present a barricade too far, even for the most liberated. Notwithstanding that we live in the post–Gloria Steinhem age, the man should go through them before the woman (so that he can do any pushing that may be required). He should not, however, go round twice in order to lead her in and follow her out, unless he wishes to appear an idiot.

RITES OF PASSAGE

Rites of passage, such as birth celebrations, weddings and funerals, all come with their own set of rules. Birth celebrations are low-key, weddings bacchanalian and funerals deferential. Try to behave accordingly.

BAR MITZVAHS

One of the most important rites in Judaism, the bar mitzvah marks a boy's passage to adulthood and is usually celebrated on the earliest convenient shabbat (Saturday) after his 13th birthday. During the ceremony, the boy recites passages of the Torah and pledges to be a good Jew. In other details, the bar mitzvah varies according to the type of synagogue in which the ceremony is held. In Orthodox temples, the men and women sit separately and must all either wear hats or cover their heads. In the most liberal Reform synagogues, almost anything goes and you may be bare-headed.

You should congratulate the bar mitzvah boy and his parents, perhaps using the term "mazel tov" (good luck).

Presents are expected, but they should not be brought to the synagogue; rather, they should be given at the party that is usually held in a different location later the same day or the next day.

Liberal Jews hold a similar event for girls; this is known as a bat mitzvah.

BIRTHS

The first news of the birth of a child is normally conveyed by the father, who calls relatives and close friends within a few hours of the arrival. The nearest and dearest will want to come and visit, but they should first find out from the father if mother and baby are well enough to bear it. If and when the well-wishers do come, they should reckon to stay only for about twenty minutes or half an hour.

Announcements

Some parents announce the birth by mailing cards. That's a good thing, but many would advise them against incorporating a photograph of the mother before she's had a chance to freshen up or of the child before he has been cleaned up. Announcements should be printed on stiffened

---

MAKING THE BIRTH ANNOUNCEMENT

If, in addition to informing people by word of mouth, the parents decide to make an announcement in a newspaper, the form of words need be no more than a bald statement of the fact:

PRIMLEY—On June 1 to Jacob
and Lucy, a son.

(There is no need to put the year—that will be at the top of the page—nor do you yet need to have decided on a name.)

Nevertheless, such notices are widely accompanied by further information that adds to the occasion:

PRIMLEY—On June 1, to Jacob and Lucy, a son,
Jason, a brother for Hector and Lucretia.

They may even stick in an epithet—"beautiful," "miraculous"—after the first indefinite article. Some people object to that practice, but there is no harm in it. Other details, such as "a long-hoped-for grandchild for Ron" may have purists muttering disapproval, but it's not their gig—if it sounds good to you, play it.

---

paper no larger than a postcard, and possibly even as small as a business card (*see page 78*), the legend should be along the lines of:

> *Jacob and Lucy Primley are happy to announce*
> *the birth of a son, Jason, on June 1, 2006.*

To that may be added, to taste, the place of birth and the child's weight.

Presents

Presents for the infant may be almost anything—from a teddy bear to a fixed-term investment fund that will mature on his 18th birthday. You've got more or less carte blanche for the mother, too: cosmetics, lotions and anything that will help her to feel feminine after her ordeal are often welcome. So too, usually, are flowers (*see also page 150*)—if they are sent to the hospital, rather than brought in person, check first to see if the mother is registered in her maiden or her married name.

Siblings

Any elder siblings may feel usurped by the new baby and resentful of what appears to be their parents' lack of concentration on the children they already have. Recognizing that, some friends and relatives give presents to the ones who fear they've been forgotten.

CHRISTENING PARTIES

There is no standard form for christening parties, but they tend to be fairly small and select events at which champagne is normally served. There should also be a christening cake, which usually resembles a baby-size wedding cake. If there is to be a proper meal, it is traditional to ask the clergyman who performed the baptism to say the grace. There is often a toast to the baby, and this may often be proposed by one of the godparents.

Guests at christening parties are expected to take presents for the child. They should wear suits or similar smart apparel.

Confirmation

Godparents are expected to attend the child's confirmation service, which, if it takes place at all, will usually happen when the child is in his early teens. Here again, a gift is expected.

Strictly speaking, the godparent's duties end when the child is confirmed. Although some adults continue sending cards and presents on the godchild's birthday and at Christmas for the rest of their lives, many take the first full communion as their cue to stop; a few carry on until the child reaches the age of majority, before they, too, decide that the ritual has run its course. Although it is all right to do that, it is important to let the child know your intention in advance. It is a rare teenager who does not take everything personally, and if his godparents suddenly and unaccountably change their giving habits after more than a decade, he might well think that it is because of something he has said or done.

Godparents

Children of Protestants usually, but not invariably, have three godparents—two of the same sex, and one of the opposite sex. In the Roman Catholic church, it is conventional to have one godparent of each sex. The father's best man is often one of the godfathers to the first male child.

Godparents receive no guidelines other than those set out on a small handbill given to them at the church on the day of the baptism. They have no legal rights, but the role carries spiritual and financial obligations. The godparent is supposed to be available any time the child may need advice or guidance. This is largely moonshine; few godparents will ever want or be in a position to knuckle in on the parents' domain.

It is an honor to be asked to be a godparent, and it is almost impossible to refuse such an invitation. It is scarcely even acceptable to decline on religious grounds, because religion no longer has very much to do with it. If you really do not want to be a godparent, the only inoffensive excuse is to say that you have so many godchildren already that you fear you will not be able to give this new one the attention he deserves. Failing that, you really have no other course than to accept graciously and ensure you make a good job of it.

Presents

Presents for godchildren are seldom easy to choose. The first gift is given on the day of the baptism and is usually an item of silverware: napkin rings, apostle spoons, forks and those absurd food pushers of which there is no recorded use in human history. Some people lay down wine or port, which will mature at about the same time as the child will first be legally permitted to drink it, but others object to this practice on the grounds that alcohol is an enemy of promise and something the child can be relied upon to discover for himself. If you want to give wine or port, ask the parents first and be prepared to take no for an answer.

For the first four or five birthdays and Christmases you can ask the parents to identify an appropriate gift; thereafter, you can get the child to tell you himself.

~

ENGAGEMENTS

When a man and a woman decide to marry, they may wish to announce the fact to interested parties. There are several ways of doing this, the most conventional of which is by taking a notice in the "Forthcoming Marriages" column of a newspaper. Whether it is a national or a local newspaper depends on whether everyone you wish to inform takes the paper in which you have chosen to advertise.

The other ways of announcing an engagement are by throwing a party or by word of mouth. Both ensure reach-

---

SHOWERS

Showers are usually held to welcome new arrivals to the community and to celebrate forthcoming marriages. The setting can be mid-morning coffee, lunch, tea, dinner or a full-blown evening bash. Invitations can be formal or informal, written or telephoned.

The idea of a shower is that guests bring presents, which can be used for the newborn or the upcoming marriage. Thus to a baby shower, everyone would be expected to bring layettes, toys and infant clothing.

Most showers involve only family and close friends—those from whom a gift would in any case be expected. Presents given at a shower held in advance of a forthcoming marriage are usually in addition to, rather than instead of, a proper wedding present.

---

ing more of the right people (that is, those you want to tell), but neither has the stylishness (to say nothing of the cachet or the snob appeal) of a newspaper advertisement. These methods are not mutually exclusive, and none is obligatory—you can always marry one day and announce the fact to your family and friends the next.

An engagement party (as distinct from a party at which an engagement is announced) is usually for only a few relatives and intimate friends, and is often the occasion of the first meeting of the bride's parents and the groom's. The only point of etiquette at an engagement party is that the bride's father may propose a toast to the couple, and the groom may reply, thanking all those present for their good wishes and proposing a toast to both sets of parents.

Announcements

The announcement of an engagement is usually organized and paid for by the bride's family. The usual form of words in a newspaper entry is this:

"The engagement is announced between Michael,
son of Mr. and Mrs. Richard Stevenson,
of Denver, Colorado, and Jennifer,
daughter of Mr. and Mrs. Kenneth Wright,
of Albany, New York."

The basic formula may be varied according to circumstance. If one parent is dead, Jennifer may be "daughter of the late Mr. Kenneth Wright and of Mrs. Annabel Wright"; if the parents are divorced, she may be "daughter of Mr. Kenneth Wright and of Mrs. Annabel Wright"; if they have subsequently remarried she may be "daughter of Mr.

Kenneth Wright and of Mrs. William Collins." The author knows of one case where the husband and wife, though still nominally married, were so estranged that they described themselves on the invitations as a divorced couple would have done. And in fact, they remain estranged ten years later, though still not divorced.

If a parent's change of surname gives rise to ambiguity about his or her relationship to the betrothed, then the child's surname should also be stated.

WEDDINGS

Best Man

The best man is the groom's wingman at the wedding. He is there to lend assistance and be like Crusoe's Man Friday. Indeed, British Royal grooms tend to call their best men "supporters," a term that describes perfectly the role of the best man.

The groom may, if he wishes, have two best men, as did Elvis Presley when he married Priscilla Beaulieu.

There is nothing to prevent a woman from being a best man. The most likely objector is of course the bride, but American divorcée Fanny Osbourne had no known misgivings when her groom, Robert Louis Stevenson, chose his friend Dora Williams to support him at their wedding in San Francisco on May 19, 1880. Stevenson later described Williams as "my guardian angel and our best man rolled into one."

Duties

The most onerous part of the best man's role is the speech in which he must toast the bride and groom, hopefully with a touch of humor, but nothing so bawdy that it will get the groom in trouble. Among the best man's other main duties are:

1) To organize and accompany the groom on the night of the bachelor party. He should ensure that the Groom gets as drunk as he wants to, and gets home in one piece.

2) To carry the wedding ring on the groom's behalf and make sure it does not get lost. A good best man will probably carry a cheap, spare ring as a stand-in in case the worst happens and the real ring falls down a drain.

3) To make sure all the groomsmen are ready before the ceremony begins.

4) To read out messages from those who were invited but unable to attend. These usually contain straight-forward messages such as "With all good wishes on your great day," but may also attempt to recycle well-worn jokes: "To the bride from the groom's softball team, 'We've tried him in every position, now it's your turn.'" A good best man will decide on the spot whether or not such gems are fit for the assembly.

Bridesmaids

The bride's attendants before, during and after the wedding ceremony are appointed by the bride and tend to be her sisters, cousins or closest friends. The bride's closest female friend is usually appointed the maid-of-honor. The bride should give them each a present either privately, after the wedding, or during the reception. If during the reception, it is usually handed over by the best man during his speech.

Civil Marriage

Civil marriages take place at City Hall or in a courthouse in front of an officiant (such as a city clerk, judge, justice of the peace or minister) and at least one witness. The ceremony can be as simple—or as complex—as the couple wishes, as long as both state that they want to marry each other. A possible vow could be:

"I take you to be my lawfully wedded husband/wife as long as we both shall live."

The register is then signed by the bride and groom, the witness and the two Registrars in front of the assembly.

Congratulations

At an engagement party or a wedding reception, you should congratulate the groom on his choice of bride. That is, you should say "Congratulations." It used to be thought unacceptable to congratulate the bride on her choice of groom, because of the overtone of entrapment it was thought to convey. Fortunately, this is one of the areas from which equal opportunities have effectively swept the cobwebs of tradition. The only rule is: gush! Gush regardless of what you really think of the tart or gigolo in question.

Groom

He appoints the best man and the ushers, he pays for the wedding ring and all expenses incurred at the place where the marriage itself takes place. He should also arrange and pay for the bride's and bridesmaids' bouquets, the bouton-nieres of his own attendants and any further flora that may be required around the place. He should also sort out the going-away transport and the honeymoon. But the above is all on the assumption that he or his parents can afford it. The financial burden can be spread around if necessary without embarrassment.

Groomsmen

The groomsmen are chosen by the groom and are usually his brothers, cousins and closest friends. Though grooms-men are traditionally male, a groom may choose a female friend or relative who is then called an honor attendant. The best man is the main groomsman, but all share in the duties of helping the husband-to-be get ready for the main event. The groomsmen may also double as ushers (*see page 141*).

Presents

If you have accepted an invitation to a wedding you must either take a present or arrange to have one sent. Presents are usually sent to the home of the bride's parents.

Many couples compile a wedding list, which they will send out on request. (Some people send it out, unsolicited, with the invitation, but that is bad form.) There are two kinds of wedding list. Sometimes the couple will go to a depart-ment store that offers a bridal registry. There, with the help of an assistant, they compile a list of the goods they need/hope to receive. They then advise guests of the shop in which the registry is held. The guests telephone, visit the shop, or look on its website, make their choice and pay the bill. The item is crossed off the list to avoid duplication of gifts.

The second method is to circulate a wedding list with no particular shop in mind. The guests should then tell the bride which item they propose to buy. She will then delete it from the list herself, and the guests will be left to make the purchase from a store of their own choice.

Another method is to have no list at all, and leave the choice entirely to the guests. Couples who adopt this course often object to a conventional wedding list on the grounds either that "we'd prefer them to buy us something personal, without any prompting," or that "it seems too much like overt soliciting."

To the first objection, the answer is that without a list you run the risk of returning from the honeymoon to a dozen toasters. To the second, the answer is more complicated. It is implicit in a wedding invitation that a party is being held at considerable expense in the expectation of a return on the investment in the form of presents. This is the financial reality.

A NO-FRILLS APPROACH

Compare the practice at a Greek Cypriot wedding. There, no presents are expected, but during the service, members of the groom's family pass among the congregation and offer boutonnieres to the male guests. Anyone who takes a flower becomes the groom's *koumbaros* (which loosely translates as something between "best man" and "sponsor"), of which there can be any number. The *koumbari* then participate in the protracted Greek Orthodox ceremonial exchange of rings. Later, at the reception, they are picked out by the family and they must then use a pin to stick money onto the groom's clothing as he dances with the bride. This is a refreshingly candid approach to what is essentially a business transaction.

In North Dakota, some couples raise money by holding an auction at the reception in which the highest bidder is permitted to remove and keep the bride's garter.

If you decline an invitation to a wedding, it is up to you whether to send a present. You may send a message—if you do, bear in mind that, by tradition, it will be read out by the best man during his speech at the reception (*see page 136*).

Rehearsal Dinner

The rehearsal dinner is held before the wedding; the date can vary from a few weeks to the day before the nuptials. It is traditionally paid for and hosted by the groom's parents. The entire cast list of the ceremony should be invited: the groom (natch) and his siblings; the bride and her parents and siblings; the grandparents on both sides; the best man, the ushers, the bridesmaids, the ring bearers, the flower girls, and the officiant who will perform the marriage. And don't forget all their husbands, wives, boyfriends and girlfriends: they should also get the pick. (Who said it was cheaper to marry off your sons than your daughters?)

Normally, the only formalities are a toast to the bride and groom, proposed by the best man, and another by the groom to his bride and her parents. After that, though, unless you're careful, it could be all-out jaw: the bride may toast her groom and his family; the groom's father may be overwhelmed by the desire to speak too; then his wife may add a few choice words…. There may be no end to it. Try not to show how transcendentally bored you are.

Ring

The bride chooses the wedding ring. The groom pays for it then keeps it till the day. It is traditional—and sometimes advisable—for the groom to give it to the best man for safe keeping on the morning of the wedding. The best man should then hand it back when they have taken their places in the church or register office.

Ushers

The ushers for the wedding are chosen by the groom, and they tend to be chosen from among his close friends and/or the brothers of the bride. Their duties are not strictly defined, but it is usual to find them performing the following necessary functions on the wedding day:

Usher 1: Hand out service sheets to the congregation at the church door. *(He may also be the backup if the best man is indisposed, incapacitated or struck dumb with terror at the prospect of public speaking.)*

Usher 2: Stand at the foot of the aisle and ask each guest "bride or groom?" meaning whose friend or relative are they. According to their reply, they will be shown to a seat either on the left of the church (bride) or the right (groom). *(Holders of this office should be warned that there will inevitably be those who answer "Both"; such guests should be directed to the side of the church which at that moment contains fewer people.)*

Both Usher 1 and Usher 2 should try to keep the back rows of the church free for latecomers; they might also suggest aisle seats for guests with young children, so that they can leave unobtrusively if the children get restless during the service.

Usher 3: Stand halfway down the aisle to seat the guests. *(Not, you may rightly assume, a vital function, but a convenient job to give someone you feel needs something to do.)*

Usher 4: Stand at the church door and escort the bride's mother to her seat on arrival. *(This may be incorporated* *into the job of Usher 1; alternatively, Usher 4 may also help Usher 1 hand out the service sheets.)*

Usher 5: organize parking of cars outside.

Who Pays

Since it is traditionally the bride's parents who pay for the wedding, they take the responsibility for organizing the venue and the press announcement, if any. It is they who compile the guest list, naturally in consultation with the groom and his parents, and send out the invitations. They also foot the bill for the reception.

However, circumstances alter cases, and there is no reason that if the bride's lot cannot afford it all the marriage cannot go ahead. In realistic practical terms, the money comes out of the account that can most easily sustain the withdrawals. Neither the groom nor his family should feel that it is a breach of etiquette to make a financial contribution.

SEPARATION AND DIVORCE

There is nothing like marriage: it is the only contract between two people that demands lifelong commitment regardless of changing circumstances, "For richer, for poorer, for better, for worse." It is so difficult that it should really not be shocking when it fails. But shocking it often is, and it is when people are taken unawares that they are most likely to say something tactless. So if a husband and wife announce that they are parting, remember never to say anything that may be construed as judgmental. Never express shock along the lines of "I always thought you two were perfect for each other," and by the same token never say "You'll be much happier now. I never liked him anyway."

In some cases—a very few—separation leads not to divorce but to reconciliation. So that's all the more reason to keep your views of the characters involved strictly to yourself.

You might want to try to pair off your newly divorced friend with someone you know to be available and whom you regard as suitable. While there is ample evidence that this sometimes works well, it is still better to tread carefully. Many divorced people have reported showing up at social occasions where they know everyone present except one, the purpose of whose presence is perfectly apparent from the moment of arrival.

The Ex-Couple

The divorced couple need to be constantly mindful that if they are going to remain in the same social circles they must behave civilly to each other in public. Arguing in the plain view of one's friends is intolerable, and it is beyond the call of duty for your host to be expected to keep an eye on you both.

If a husband and wife decide to separate they should let all their relatives and friends know about it as quickly as they can. That doesn't always come easily—they are distraught and reluctant to discuss personal matters with outsiders—but it's a matter that needs to be addressed. The information is often imparted in a note that accompanies the Christmas card—not ideal at the time of peace on Earth and good will to all men, but since many people only communicate in writing at this time of year I suppose there's little alternative. Certainly there are few people who will want to write personal letters on the subject to all their friends.

The Friends

If a couple divorces and you liked only one of the parties, the way forward is clear: drop the other like a stone. If you liked them both, you will, in the future, have to consider the social consequences. If you have a party and invite them both, you should tell each that the other may be coming. This can be done by phone or in a note with the invitation.

Maiden Name

After a divorce, the woman may revert to her maiden name. More usually, however, she keeps her married surname but is henceforth known not as Mrs. Henry Tudor but as Mrs. Catharine Tudor. Which is just what she would have done if she had been widowed.

DEATH AND CONDOLENCE

The best expressions of sympathy—both written and spoken—show understanding of the relationship between the addressee and the dead person.

It is common for people who have lost loved ones to reproach themselves with thoughts that they might have done more for the deceased, that they should have been there for him when they were needed, and even that the death itself may somehow have been averted by their presence. Any happiness that the bereaved may have brought the deceased should therefore be emphasized as much as possible. It is good to say or write, if you can do so in good conscience, that the bereaved were indispensable to the dead person, that they improved the quality of his life, or even that they saw the deceased as much as possible during life.

It is also good to dwell on your own pleasant memories of the dead person—reminiscence is good, especially if it is a nice story which the addressee will not already know.

Anyone who has lost parents or siblings may fear that whatever killed them may also come for him. If you know of anything—debilitating childhood illness or graduate work with plutonium—which might be taken as a fairly sure sign that history will not repeat itself, it were well to mention it.

Sympathetic people should try to ensure that the bereaved have plenty to occupy them and little opportunity to become even lower of spirit through excessive introspection.

Bad Memories

If you knew something bad about the deceased and you didn't tell anyone about it in his lifetime, let him take your secret to the grave. The reminiscences that appear in the *Times* over the days following the main obituary invariably celebrate the qualities of the dead person; they do not dwell on his shortcomings, sins and outrages.

It is not acceptable to say that the deceased wasted his talent or that he was a good-for-nothing, especially if it's the truth.

SOCIAL EVENTS

This section deals with ways in which a host should notify people of his forthcoming social functions, how guests should respond to invitations, and what preparations the host and guests need to make before the event. Also included are tips about how guests should conduct themselves.

BARBECUES

Barbecues, by their nature, are casual affairs. However, that does not mean you shouldn't follow some simple rules to keep guests comfortable and relaxed.

- Try to ensure that there is shade in your backyard and that there are enough seats for everyone present. If one or both is impossible, don't discourage guests from taking their food indoors.
- Garden torches filled with citronella oil can be burned to keep insects away from sweet food and drink.
- Make sure all the drinks are cold, and that you have both alcoholic and non-alcoholic choices. Low-calorie drinks, such as diet soda, are also a thoughtful addition for those who may be watching their weight.
- Offer at least one vegetarian option.
- If you are barbecuing at home, be sure to invite your neighbors. Don't make them feel like starving peasants watching you feast on the castle side of the moat.

BIRTHDAYS

Some people like to push the boat out as far as it will go on these occasions; others find little cause for rejoicing in the passage of time and do little or nothing to mark the appearance of yet another ring around the trunk. In a pluralistic society, there are no grounds for criticizing either approach. If you accept an invitation to a birthday party, don't show up empty-handed.

COCKTAIL PARTIES

A cocktail party is usually held in the early evening and can be almost anything the host wishes it to be. Although dinner will not be served, there may be "nibbles" (canapés, sandwiches, small sausages and the like).

Invitations may be telephoned, but if they are printed or written they should say simply "Cocktails 5–7 p.m." together with the date of the party. They should also have "R.S.V.P." with the host's name, address and phone number in the bottom left hand corner of the card.

CRASHING THE PARTY

If you have God-like understanding and forgiveness of your fellow men, you may not detest those who crash your party—you may even take it as a compliment that they should wish to appear at a function they were not asked to attend. Most people are not so charitable. However, the temptation to say "If I'd known you were coming, I'd have invited you" should be resisted. You will probably have to bite the bullet and pretend you're delighted to see them. If guests ask beforehand if they can bring so-and-so, feel free to say no—unless of course you want so-and-so and had simply forgotten him or didn't know he was in the country.

If someone you have invited turns up with someone else you have not, again you'll have to deal with it, but you'll know who not to ask next time.

DANCING

Men have always been able to ask women to dance, but now women can ask men without embarrassment. If the person asked doesn't want to, he or she should not say "No." It were better to recall Proverbs 15, i, "A soft answer turneth away wrath," and say something like "I'd rather sit this one out, if you don't mind."

GIFTS

Whatever the occasion—birthday, wedding or anniversary—the ground rules are clear: try to give something the recipient will want, but if you can't think of anything, give something impressive and/or expensive. Still it's much the best course to give something useful or of personal significance, even if it costs very little.

Gift cards are a good choice, even though they let the recipient know how much they cost. Some people think such presents show a lack of thought, but that is a mistake: a gift card for a famous store has cachet and carries no attendant danger of duplicating someone else's gift. The only proviso is that people who live in the boonies may not have much occasion to shop at Gucci, so care has to be exercised over the proximity of the recipient to the shop.

If the hosts insist that they want nothing, don't be annoyed. In case you really want or feel you ought to give them a gift, make it something that will go in an envelope, which you can keep about your person—tickets to some event, perhaps. Then you can arrive empty-handed yet not feel uncomfortable. Alternatively, you can send flowers to arrive just before or just after the event.

However, most visitors will feel more at ease if they do not enter the house empty-handed. If you can't think of anything particularly apt for the occasion, that is where chocolates or flowers come in.

To those who have everything, give flowers. For children you don't know, money may be better than an irrelevance. If you send flowers or a present to a wedding you don't attend and you never get an acknowledgement, you should come out and ask. They may have been lost in the mail or the store from which you ordered them may have made a mistake.

Receiving Gifts

When presented with gifts, the hostess should quickly take a view on what to do with them. If they're obviously edible or drinkable, she should put them close by to be served at the appropriate moment—chocolates, for example, should be served after dinner. If she's been presented with a very good wine, she should ask the guest what he wants done with it—should I drink it now, or save it for another occasion? (A good guest will endeavor to answer this question before it is asked.) In the case of flowers, it is probably better not to flap around arranging them there and then, but to stick them in the nearest vase or sink and put them out only after everyone has gone home. If it's a personal gift, the giver should suggest that the recipient might like to open it later. By the same token, if the size of the gift puts the recipient in fear that she will have to spend half an hour unwrapping, cooing and thanking—time better spent on getting the evening going and serving the food—she should say "Thanks, do you mind if I open it later?" and pop it away.

Wine

Guests above a certain age (typically, those who are older than college students or those beyond their first job) need not take bottles of wine to parties. There is no rule about this—if you've got some particularly toothsome vintage you wish to share, don't be inhibited. But it's better to take no wine than a bottle of something cheap and nasty.

Hosts are expected to be able to afford their own booze, their tastes may be different from yours, and the wine you choose may not be appropriate for the meal. In some countries it's regarded as an insult to take wine because to do so implies that the hostess can't be relied upon to organize such things herself.

HOUSEWARMING PARTIES

Housewarming parties are informal events, announced by phone or e-mail rather than invitation cards. If you're going to one you're expected to take a present: a Monet would be nice, but a plant would do. You should also gush about the newly acquired property, and don't make the mistake of thinking that "It sure has a lot of potential" will be taken to mean anything other than "You paid for this?"

~

INVITATIONS

It is tactful and wise not to put invitations you have received on the mantelpiece or anywhere they are likely to be seen by mutual friends who may not have been asked.

If your children do not appear on the invitation, you may take it that they are not invited and it would be a violation of etiquette to call and ask the host for clarification of this point.

Advance Warning

If you are holding any sort of get-together, it is important to get the length of notice about right. If you give too

---

WORDING AN INVITATION

Printed invitations may be styled in the third person—for example:

Mr. and Mrs. Jacob Primley request the pleasure of your company at a party to celebrate

Lucy's birthday

The Langham Hotel, London W1
Saturday, July 4th, 7:30 p.m.
Black tie

RSVP

The legend should give the occasion (Lucy's birthday), the location (The Langham), the date and the time. Don't forget to mention any dress requirements. The name of the recipient should be written by hand in the top left-hand corner of the card.

---

much, the guests may think it's a very grand affair; moreover they might forget about it in the intervening period. If you give too little warning, you may cause offense to those who think they're just emergency fill-ins. You may give people longer to make up their minds in certain circumstances, especially if the proposed function is to be held during a peak holiday period.

The rules of thumb are as follows:

- people you don't know very well should be given about two weeks' notice.
- strangers or VIPs or busy people should be allowed longer, perhaps as long as a month.
- close friends need no notice, but don't push your luck.

At Home

When this appears on an invitation, it means that you don't need to take a bottle of wine with you unless you are specifically asked to do so. Dress smartly.

Invitation Cards

In this unbuttoned age, it no longer much matters whether invitation cards are printed or engraved. Nevertheless, sticklers for convention prefer engraved cards; these are more expensive but look more impressive. Invitation cards were once addressed to the wife, but that is no longer necessary. (Sympathy cards, incidentally, need not be black-edged.)

Minuses

Instead of RSVP, some invitations say "Regrets only." So if you are going, you can put the money you saved by not having to reply to the host into a better present.

Pluses

Some party throwers write "John Smith plus one" (alternatively "+1"), or "plus friend" or "and family." The absence of such addenda means that John Smith should show up alone. Some people disapprove of "+1" on the grounds of impersonality: if you don't know the name, don't invite the person, even if it is a good friend of a friend. However, this only applies to formal, grown-up events. If you're having a cocktail party or some other casual bash, "+1" is fine. It is also fine if the person you're inviting is likely to change companions without you necessarily being up-to-date with the latest developments.

❧

LEAVING

How long are guests expected to stay at a function? This can sometimes be stated on the invitation without causing offense. It is not rude to put "6:30–8:00"; it is just cultural shorthand for "Dinner will not be served." Normally, lunch should be over by 3 p.m. Dinner guests should make noises about leaving at about 11:30 p.m. and aim to be out of the door by midnight unless they are pressed to stay.

❧

POTLUCKS

Potlucks are parties to which one is expected to bring food to share with all the other guests. Though I am not a fan of such functions, it is a perfectly acceptable American tradition.

While it may be presumptuous to assign specific dishes to those invited (beef Wellington from you, Janice), it's fine to give general guidelines or else you may end up with four apple pies, five bags of chips and nothing else. A sign-up sheet is a good way to ensure all the "groups" are covered: appetizers, entrées, side dishes and desserts. The holder of the potluck is traditionally responsible for the drinks.

If you are a guest, whatever you take should be ready to eat on arrival: there should be no reheating. Remember to take your empty dish home when you leave; if you forget the dirty container, it is your responsibility to pick it up from the host's home.

TOASTS

A toast may come at the end of a speech or when someone grabs the group's attention (often by standing up, sometimes by tapping his glass with an item of cutlery, occasionally by voice projection and force of personality). It starts with a proposal, which is invariably an expression of good will. It may simply be "Cheers"; it may be dedicated to a particular person or persons ("The bride and groom"); it may be in anticipation of a desired outcome ("Peace on Earth") or in celebration of an achievement ("Nelson Mandela, Nobel laureate"). The other people present then raise their glasses (they may also clink each other's, if they are within easy reach), repeat the key phrase in unison, and take a sip. The drink need not be alcohol, but the superstitious, including sailors, proscribe the use of water, which is thought to portend a watery grave.

MUSIC

No matter how great the temptation to use music at social functions as an ice-breaker, to cover silences or dampen the noise of punch-ups or the drone of bones, it should not be played as background for a formal occasion, especially a formal meal. If it's good music, it should be listened to with full attention; if it's not good music it should not be heard at all.

The above is not intended to preclude social events with musical interludes: you can have dancing or a band, certainly, but make sure in the former case that there is a quiet room for those who don't do terpsichore, and in the latter that the performers get a fair hearing—you don't want to send the musicians home with the feeling that they'd have been better appreciated in the subway.

SEATING PLAN

One of the host's greatest advantages is that he can fix the seating plan to ensure that he is next to the most interesting guest and as far as possible away from the biggest bore. Apart from that, the main rule is to keep husbands and wives apart at the table. Some authorities say that lovers should be seated next to each other, but experience dictates that it is better to treat such couples as married than to have them feeling each other up under the table while you're trying to scintillate the assembly with your repartee. The most important male guest should be seated on the host-

---

POOR CIRCULATION

Normally the host shouldn't leave another guest on his own. But that only works if people circulate, and let's face it they seldom do. So if you get marooned, and you can't even wave to passing ships, you've just got to pretend that the person with whom you're stuck is the companion you would have chosen if you'd had a scintilla of free will. If no one comes to rescue you, your only hopes are if your cell rings or if you really are in desperate need of the loo. But it has to be a real emergency.

---

ess's right, and the most important female should be placed on the right of the host. Thence it should be man–woman–man–woman around the table.

At a large dinner party you will usually talk to the person seated on your immediate left or right. In the happy event that you find each other agreeable and talk until the end of the main course, remember the guest on your other side and talk to him during the dessert.

If you are expected to change seats for dessert, talk to one side during the starter and the other during the main. Unless, of course, either party is inextricably engrossed with the person on the far side.

❧

VISITING

After ringing the doorbell, it is conventional to get off the doorstep and wait there until someone answers. (Just one step, that is; if the entrance is at the top of a flight, you are not expected to beat the retreat.) This is a wise course of action in case the householder should spring out at you like a Jack-in-the-box with a clenched fist or an offensive weapon. In earlier times, callers would retire to a safe distance to avoid attack by castellans who might pour boiling oil from the battlements onto the heads of the medieval equivalents of encyclopedia salesmen and Jehovah's Witnesses.

TECHNIQUETTE

It was from Bobby Ewing, a character in *Dallas*, a popular television series of the late 1970s and early 1980s, that I first heard the axiom "Conversation is a two way street." Since actor Patrick Duffy delivered that daft but evidently memorable line, the thoroughfare to which he referred has been widened into a multilane superhighway by a technological revolution that has made cell phones, e-mail and Black-berries part of many people's everyday lives. Such innovations have raised various new questions of etiquette.

ANSWERING MACHINES & VOICEMAIL

It is a violation of etiquette to ring and not leave a message. The sole exception to this rule is in cases where you have got a wrong number. An even worse fault is to leave a message when you know before you call that the other person is going to be out and then assume that the onus is on him to get back to you. It may keep the phone bill down, but it's mighty annoying.

It is maddening to have to listen to recorded messages that are supposed to be funny. One irritating young man taped part of Edvard Grieg's incidental music for *Peer Gynt* over which he was to be heard saying "This is the Hall of the Mountain King. I'm afraid the Mountain King is not available at the moment…."

CELL PHONES

If a person has only one phone and that phone is a cell, it is difficult to adduce cogent reasons why he should not make and receive calls in public places as well as at home. However, it is aesthetically repugnant to have to endure the sight and sound of people using mobiles in any milieu which, but for their presence, would be perfectly unblighted by the telephone. A telephone conversation is a form of intimacy, not a spectator sport. It is regrettable that some people take and make mobile telephone calls in public in an attempt to show the uninterested world how busy and important they are. As for people who let them ring during theatrical performances, there is no fate too awful.

If you're going into a meeting or a movie or a theater performance, you will of course turn off your cell at the entrance. But in restaurants most people leave them on. While the cell was still new-fangled I did wonder how bad it would be to answer mine at lunch if it rang and the display showed the name of anyone other than a caller of the highest conceivable importance. But since then I've been to so many such events at which fellow diners have taken calls that I've become convinced that it is not a heinous thing to do. Certainly I've never been offended. All you need to do is avoid making calls yourself, and ensure that you spend more than half the time at the table concentrating on the corporeal presences that are with you.

The only real objection to the use of cell phones on public transportation is the low quality of the ensuing dia-

---

AN ACTOR DESPAIRS

In 2004, actor Richard Griffiths responded angrily to a member of the audience whose phone had gone off six times during a performance of *The History Boys* at The National Theatre in London. He came to the front of the stage, pointed at the perpetrator, and told him: "Go, and never come back." In November 2005, he rose again after a phone rang in the audience for the third time during a performance of *Heroes* at the Wyndham's Theatre. He stepped out of part and demanded: "Is that it, or will it be ringing some more?" Warming to his theme, he reportedly continued, "Could the person whose mobile it is please leave? The 750 people here would be fully justified in suing you for ruining their afternoon."

---

logue. It's not that one expects a torrent of epigrams, merely that, even as statements of the obvious go, "I'm on a train" is dramatic irony of the lowest imaginable order. And it would help if they didn't talk like they were making a public announcement.

Ring Tones

If you suddenly find that a snatch of music has lodged itself unaccountably in your brain and will not be banished, you may well have gotten it from someone else's cell phone ring tone. After a decade of the Overture to Bizet's *Carmen*, "La donna é mobile" from Verdi's *Rigoletto* and others, there are now welcome signs of a long overdue backlash against such irritating tunes. Despite the fact that some people have downloaded "Who Let the Dogs Out," others—the cultural elite?—have adopted the tone of the old traditional Bakelite phone in the hall. So there's hope of peace for the rest of us.

~

E-MAIL

E-mail is full of traps, not the least of which is that it is superficially a more informal medium than the traditional paper letter. Many people send each other dirty jokes and rude attachments electronically, not only from their own PCs but also through work. If you are not certain that such material will be welcomed, don't send it.

Be on your guard about what you write and the way you express yourself. Letters begin with "Dear So-and-So" and end with "Yours faithfully" or "Yours sincerely," e-mails

OTHER E-MAIL RULES

- Don't use the exclamation mark high-priority flag as a matter of course.
- Avoid the use of block capitals, PEOPLE SAY IT'S SHOUTING. Exclamation marks are also to be avoided, as they are in real letters.
- Check what's written on the subject line, if it really is a reply, leave in the "Re:" if it's to the same person but about something else, put in a new header.
- Add disclaimers that make it clear that not everything written by an employee is company policy.
- Think about cc-ing and replying to all: do they really need to know this?
- Be careful about forwarding a message. Does the person to whom you're intending to send it really want or need to know?
- Don't forward chain letters about ways of getting money out of Bill Gates and fortunes from frozen bank accounts in Nigeria.
- Warnings about viruses are seldom useful and usually extremely boring.
- Don't e-mail confidential material; write a proper letter or arrange a meeting.
- Don't let the spell-check fool you into avoiding the passive voice, if he was killed, how else do you say it?

typically begin with "Hi," but that doesn't mean that the person addressed is your best friend, or would ever want to be. They normally end with just the name of the sender, and sometimes not even that, because it is after all on the top line. You can use a valediction if you wish, but it's neither usual nor expected.

Informal e-mails can be as informal as you like or think you can get away with, but business e-mails should stick to the rules of normal, old-style paper correspondence: let them begin with "Dear So-and-So" and end with "Sincerely," "Yours faithfully," "Best wishes," "Yours truly" or whatever.

Never make the mistake of thinking that e-mail is private. Be careful what you say, and be ever mindful of the ease with which rude remarks can be forwarded—accidentally or accidentally on purpose—to the person being insulted.

Strings of Initials

Don't use abbreviations such as "AFAIK: (as far as I know) "OTOH" (on the other hand), "IYAM" (if you ask me) and so on. They're not clever and they're not smart, they're just annoying to those who don't know what they mean and boring to those who do. They're okay on text messages, but nowhere else.

Automatic Replies

Templates for frequently used responses can save you a lot of time and effort, but they may annoy those who receive them. It is in general better to keep someone waiting a week for a full and considered answer to his queries or problems than to send a "Thank you for your communication" type reply. Most people have great confidence in e-mail—if they send a message and it doesn't get returned, they assume it's got through. Automatic "out of the office" responses can get trapped in a loop—two machines tell each other a thousand times that the query will be dealt with on their users' return from vacation.

Attachments

If you need to attach files, tread carefully—it's often better to check if the intended recipient can read the program

TEXT ABBREVIATIONS

You get a message and it's full of abbreviations that you don't understand. Is the sender rudely presumptuous, or are you completely clueless? I don't know the answer to that, but these are some of the most commonly used groups of initials whose meaning may not immediately be obvious to the uninitiated

aml	all my love
atm	at the moment
bbl	be back later
bff	best friends forever
brb	be right back
btw	by the way
cul8r	see you later
fyeo	for your eyes only
hwc	handle with care
lmao	laughing my ass off
lol	lots of love (or laugh out loud: context is all)
oic	oh I see
omg	oh my God
rofl	rolling on the floor laughing
tb	text back
tbs	text back soon
ttyl	talk to you later
tks	thanks
umbj	you must be joking

you're thinking of sending than to unleash a dirty great document that may take half an hour to download and then be unopenable.

Language

Don't tie yourself in knots about gender-neutral language. Some people are offended by the use of masculine pronouns when they may refer to females. Hence a sentence such as "All we are asking is that every child should learn from his experience" may be changed to "All we are asking is that every child should learn from his or her experience." The problem with that is that the user ends up having to mention both sexes in all his/her writing, ending up with a page full of forward slashes that may end up driving him/her wo/mental. The elegant way out of this is to use the plural passim: "All we are asking is that children should learn from experience."

Mind your language, and bear in mind that some companies have filters that will refuse anything deemed to be potentially offensive. I had an e-mail bounced back from a very straight-laced company because the correspondence referred to a football club named Arsenal. If I'd written about Scunthorpe United, would they have called the police?

Avoid in-house jargon for members of the public: you may call your Ways and Means Building Organisation by the acronym WAMBO, but it's unfair to expect anyone outside the company to know what you're going on about.

∾

P.A. SYSTEMS

How soon do a microphone and a captive audience turn a normally harmless person into a homicidal bore. Remember that all art aspires to the condition of music, not to that of disc jockeys. Keep your announcements and speeches short and sweet.

~

TELEPHONE

It is incumbent upon the person who makes the call to be forthcoming with information first. Do not ring a number and immediately demand to know to whom you are speaking; it is up to you to identify yourself. If you're ringing A at B's house and B answers the phone, it is as well to sound apologetic about bothering him. Keep any messages you may wish to leave with B for A short.

When you answer your own phone, say "Hello." If you're especially benevolent you might say your name, but why should you when it might be a heavy breather who's misdialed and likes the sound of your voice? If someone calls you and says, "Is this 456-7890?" and it isn't, that is all they need to be told, they do not need to know your correct number.

If a caller asks to speak to someone other than yourself, normally the polite thing to do is to hand the phone over immediately to the person requested. If, on the other hand, you have the job of fielding calls for someone who will speak to caller A but doesn't want to hear from caller B, you may have to find out the caller's name.

"May I ask who's calling?"
is the perfect form of words.

"May I ask what it's about?"
however, is nosy and invites a flea in the ear.

Anyone unfortunate enough to be asked this impertinent question should politely deflect it by saying "It's a per-

---

UNSOLICITED CALLS FROM TELEMARKETERS

Some people say that you should tolerate the heaving of such rocks into the pool of your domestic tranquillity at the most inconvenient times (just as the roast is being carved for a Sunday dinner) since most of the callers are impoverished youths trying to make an honest buck. While torrents of abuse are discourteous and do not in my experience even get your number removed from their lists, it is surely no bad thing to say "Not interested" and put the phone down. If call centers did not exist, it would not be necessary to invent them, and students would find other ways of eking out their tuition.

---

sonal matter." This response will do even if it's obviously a business call and you've never met whoever it is.

If you're a guest in someone's home and you need to use his phone, ask for permission first.

Missed a Call?

You miss a call; you dial the "last number" function (★69); you don't recognize it; you ring the caller. What do you say when you get an answer? Your own name and "did you just call me?" If you omit the former you're inviting the response "I don't know, who are you?" and soon you find you're on a war footing before you realize it's your oldest friend from an unfamiliar phone.

Let Your Fingers Do the Walking

At work, dial your calls yourself—don't instruct underlings to do it for you. In some firms it is regarded as good practice to say your own name when you answer the phone. While that seems unnatural to me—why should you give away such precious information before you know whether you're dealing with a friend or a foe?—I have never worked for anyone who insisted on it, and if I had I am sure I would just have done as I was asked.

Let's Chat

Even if you've got time to kill shooting the breeze on the phone, don't assume that the other person is at a similarly loose end. Ask if now is a good time. And even if you get an affirmative response, don't jump to the conclusion that he is up for the full 140 minutes.

MISCELLANEOUS

This chapter includes manners for discussion that would appear on a meeting agenda under the heading Any Other Business. They are neither more nor less important than the other material in this book; they have merely proved harder to categorize. Again the reader may either follow the guidelines or scoff at the very idea of them. But if you take the latter course you should be aware that some people set great store by such rules and may judge you on your choices. If you don't care about any of that, fair play to you as they say in Ireland: just so long as you know that you'll be branded by some as a wild card or a dissident.

BODY PIERCINGS AND TATTOOS

A paradox: such adornments are intended at least in part as conversation starters, but what is there to say about them? A courteous man would not normally tell a woman with a ring through her nose that he'd like to tie a rope through it and drag her off somewhere quiet, even or especially if that's what's really on his mind. Neither would one be well advised to ask a man with "Jessica" in a heart etched indelibly on his forearm if he was still seeing the lady in the legend. It's also poor to ask people with visible tattoos if they have others elsewhere, in more intimate places—not because the answer wouldn't be interesting, but because it's too obvious and trite a gambit.

If you have tattoos, many people will regard you as potentially dangerous, so bear in mind that body art might not play well in certain contexts (job interviews; picking up children from preschool; etc.).

DRIVING

On the road, almost no one drives badly deliberately or maliciously. So don't go on about women drivers, and don't complain that the lights are always against you; they're not, and over a lifetime it will all even out.

Asking Directions

Whoever came up with the motto "Real men don't ask for directions" was a moron and should be dropped off in the middle of the Mojave desert and allowed to find his own way out. A real man knows when he is lost and is willing to admit it. Everyone makes mistakes. The difference between a boy and a man is that a man recognizes his and takes the necessary steps to correct them.

The Horn

There are situations where the horn is necessary such as when your vehicle is moving and you need to warn other road users of your presence. However, never sound your horn aggressively or in response to what you may think was an inconsiderate move by another motorist. Research shows no evidence that any traffic jam has ever been cleared by sounding the horn.

Personalized License Plates

If you really want people to know who you are, why don't you put your name on the windshield and rear bumper rather than pay a premium for a license plate that may be ostentatious, ludicrously contrived, and probably both?

Road Rage

Road rage is both uncouth and dangerous. Getting frustrated and venting your anger on other drivers will not make you arrive at your destination any sooner. It will merely reveal you to be someone who cannot control his emotions.

Turn Signals

People who do not signal their intentions by the conventional method are annoying, but they have not necessarily declared war on society. They are merely so full of themselves that they assume that anything they do is the obvious and right course of action, and that they have no need to forewarn others or justify themselves.

What Do You Drive?

In a sane world a car would be nothing more than a means of transport. In the real one it is often the owner's personal statement. No one can quite hear what he is saying, but he is definitely trying to tell us something about his means and his status. Since a man's car may be admired, envied or deplored by his fellows, his choice is to some degree influenced by manners: how does he want to come across? Does he want to dominate the swelling scene or remain part of the backdrop?

Men and women of taste and discernment do not seek status symbols; they drive the car that most closely fulfills their requirements within their price bracket. But many people wish to impress and cow others with the cost, size and classiness of their "autostable." Others are afraid of being ridiculed by their friends for being seen in a jalopy. For all such persons, the choice of the right car—or, at least, the avoidance of the wrong one—is crucial to the preservation of social standing.

Some vehicles move in and out of fashion more nimbly than ever they negotiate urban congestion, but many cars continually struggle to escape stereotyping. Any bore will tell you that Italian cars "rot like pears"; it is conventional (although increasingly anachronistic) to deplore the build quality and image of Korean vehicles.

You would be wise to be unimpressed by the level of debate on this subject. If, on the other hand, you are concerned to avoid being damned by association with your car, it may be worth noting some of the criticisms that follow.

The eco-chic Toyota Prius is the hallmark of the neo-hippie who wants the world to know he cares about the environment. Away from the green part of the spectrum, it's all about excess, flash and hip-hop style for those who choose Cadillac Escalades with spinning 24-inch rims.

A Corvette may say speed and performance, but it also implies "mid-life crisis." Can't afford Chevy's top sports car? Buy a Camaro, the poor man's Corvette.

The Honda Civic defined the sport compact market; the Ford Focus is a pale imitation of its Japanese counterpart. But for reliability, there's always the Toyota Camry (read: boring housewife car).

Inverted snobs sometimes go for motorized tin cans that have some cachet because they are cheap and spartan. The East German Trabant, which was a two-stroke joke throughout its time as a production model, became highly desirable almost as soon as it was discontinued after the collapse of Communism.

French cars tend to have more style than substance, and even their elegance may be vitiated by such idiosyncrasies as a foot-operated handbrake. German cars have few detractors, and most Porsches, Audis, Mercedes and Volkswagens are fit to grace driveways almost anywhere.

ELEVATORS

People make a great show of not looking at each other, and normally face the door throughout their period of confinement in an elevator. Anyone who breaks either of these rules, or worse attempts to start a conversation, has other occupants of the box reaching nervously for their cell phones or Mace spray.

When entering a public elevator, nod politely if you happen to make eye contact with a passenger, but do not attempt to strike up a lively dialogue. If the elevator is in your apartment building and a neighbor is sharing the ride, you would not be overstepping the boundaries of privacy by exchanging a few pleasantries.

NEIGHBORS

In a perfect world there would be enough room between ourselves and our neighbors for us to play our music whenever we liked but not so many miles that we slept with one eye open for fear that if we were burgled no one would hear us scream.

Many of us, however, live cheek by jowl, separated by paper-thin party walls. The most mundane sounds are likely to carry farther than they're meant to go. In apartments, even a toilet flush may be audible next door; this may be irritating, but it were folly to complain, since man has an inalienable right to relieve pressure on his bowel and bladder. In gardens, our trees may overhang next door's land (the neighbor either objects to them or picks their fruit); our kids kick balls halfway along the street; they may even break other people's windows.... The list of activities that, while innocuous in themselves, can drive a neighbor crazy, is almost endless. If you have to have someone living next door to you, these are a few of the simple things you can do to avoid pissing him off.

- If you're having a party or, particularly, a barbecue at home, invite him.
- If you must play loud music, do it at civilized times (perhaps no earlier than 9 a.m. and no later than 11 p.m.), and make sure your windows are closed when you do. That applies to all forms: Brahms can be every bit as maddening as Eminem if you didn't want to listen to him.
- If he's going away, offer to keep an eye on his place; even if he'd rather accept a night's lodging with Macbeth, it's the thought that counts.
- Try to make your pets as inoffensive as possible. Dogs bark, but they can still be discouraged from howling at the moon; they defecate, too, but you can train them to do it in noncontentious locations, and you can take responsibility for any mistakes by clearing them up. Cats are unherdable, but their rampagings can be constrained by shutting them out of certain areas.
- Don't have loud and lengthy conversations with third parties on your doorstep or through your windows: either ask your interlocutor in or get him to move along.
- If you're planning construction or remodeling to your house that might cause disruption, let your neighbor know in advance. But for legal reasons make sure

you're only informing him as a courtesy rather than asking his permission; if you need the latter, get it through an attorney.

- If you get his misdirected mail, just drop it off quickly. Don't return to sender, and make sure you don't let it lie around for months in your house.

- If you have to talk to him about a specific matter, and there is no impending social event you'll both be attending at which you can just drop it into conversation, you'll have to call him or knock on his door. In either case, when he answers—and this is perhaps the golden rule—don't assume that he'll want to schmooze for hours.

Those of the above points that involve dialogue depend on the neighbor himself being faintly civilized. But even if he isn't, you should extend him every courtesy.

❧

PUBLIC RESTROOMS

At the stalls, males should look straight ahead or straight down; their gaze must never stray to left or right. Do not go to a urinal directly next to one that is already in use unless there is no other option. Take care when washing your hands—if there's a sudden spurt of water from the tap, you may end up with splashmarks that make you appear guilty of a crime you have not committed.

Women's restrooms, I am told, are altogether freer and easier venues. The main complaint is that they generally don't feature sufficient cubicles to meet demand. But that's a civic matter, not a problem of etiquette.

PUBLIC TRANSPORTATION

Although it's not impossible that you will make a lifelong friend on a bus, airplane or train journey, it is much more likely that you will antagonize your fellow travelers. If you want to keep out of trouble, the following are some things you should think seriously about not dreaming of doing:

1) Talk to the person next to you.
2) Touch anyone, no matter how crowded the conveyance.
3) Play music through headphones so loudly that others can hear it.
4) Eat. Exceptions may be made for sweets, but recently microwaved meals are out of order; you are not in the dining car of The Orient Express.
5) Drop chewing gum or stick it on the furnishings.
6) Drink anything other than water or maybe tea or coffee from a thermos.
7) Sing.
8) Ask for money.
9) If you are male, sit with your legs spread so far apart that no one can comfortably occupy the adjacent seat.
10) Anything overtly sexual, alone or with others.

SHARING AN APARTMENT

1) Pay your share in full and on time.
2) Don't take the last of anything without replacing it immediately.

3) Rinse the bath after use.

4) Put everything back where you found it.

5) Regard your roommates' bedrooms as inviolable sanctuaries.

6) Leave everything—particularly the sink and the toilet—as you would wish to find it.

7) Don't leave your impedimenta strewn around the common areas.

8) If you ignore Point 7, don't be resentful or harbor grudges when your stuff disappears or gets broken by a vandal whom you never identify.

9) Don't move your partner in as a full-time non-paying extra tenant.

10) Remember that the apartment-sharing arrangement isn't permanent; drop anchor, but don't take root.

∿

SMOKING

It has long been known that smoking is harmful. King James the First and Sixth was wise to it in the early 17th century, and he didn't make the discovery himself. Since this ancient wisdom became enshrined on cigarette packets it has been open season on smokers; anyone is licensed to be prejudiced against them. They are a widely persecuted dying breed. It is every bit as much a violation of etiquette to harass nicotine addicts as it is for smokers themselves to smoke in someone else's house without permission.

During a Meal

While dining, do not smoke between courses unless everyone present is a committed smoker. Never smoke while another person at your table is still eating. If you are some-one's guest in a restaurant and you need cigarettes, ask the waiter and pay for them there and then. Don't allow your host to subsidize your bad habits.

At any restaurant that allows smoking, diners are asked on arrival whether they'd prefer the smoking or the non-smoking section. This is fine so long as customers are will-ing to believe the fantasy that the smoke produced in the permitted area will obediently turn back at the frontier, the unguarded line in the linoleum. The difficulty is that if you reply that you don't mind, they don't know where to put you. In this as in other areas of life, notably marketing sur-veys, it is undesirable to coerce people into expressing a preference when they have none.

Brother, Can You Spare a Smoke?

In a world where everyone is trying to quit but has not yet quite managed it, recalcitrant smokers find that all sorts of people—close friends and complete strangers alike—ask them for cigarettes in bars, after dinner, even in the street. I have known committed smokers who as far as I can tell have never bought a pack in their lives. Since it is discour-teous to refuse, it is the duty of scroungers to ensure that they occasionally put back a bit of what they have taken.

Cigars and Pipes

Cigar and pipe smokers should be at particular pains to ensure that their habits are not making their neighbors nauseous. The quality of most smells is subjective, but there is a broad consensus that cigarettes are the least worst form of tobacco.

Second-Hand Smoke

Smokers should make every effort not to envelop others in their fog. Nonsmokers, for their part, should remember that, while everyone now knows it's a bad habit, it is not an evil or illegal practice, and they have no license to deal with addicts as if they were pedophiles or violent revolutionaries. The treatment currently meted out to poor wheezing drug dependents in social and public contexts sometimes looks like a prelude to having them lynched. Passive smoking may be risky, but so is crossing the street: just live and let die.

XENOPHOBIA

Although some of us find it an enormous imaginative leap, we should enter all dealings with foreigners on the assumption that they are almost as human and intelligent as ourselves. Some pundits will advise against mentioning the Second World War to Germans; a serious 20th-century guidebook warned visitors to Lisbon not to talk about the earthquake which destroyed much of the city in 1764 because it's still a sore point.

This is eyewash, eyewash is offensive, and causing offense is a violation of etiquette. It is important to remember that all generalizations are false, and reference to "the Spanish temperament" implies that they've only got one between them all. A remark like "He's Mexican, you know" is likely to be insulting by implication, but certain to be explicitly meaningless, an unintelligible shorthand. Before making rash, dim-witted and offensive remarks about someone who is identifiably different from you, try substituting

---

SOCIAL SITUATION

You meet a friend of a friend for a drink and you ask him, as you do, "How is work?" And he replies: "It's okay apart from all the kikes." For a moment you can't think what to say; he sees you demur and adds quickly, "You're not Jewish, are you?"

How should you respond? Should you:

(a) Say yes (regardless of the facts)?
(b) Say no (ditto)?
(c) Push him through a plateglass window?
(d) Walk out without a further word?

The short answer is I don't know either. (a) is too combative: remember you have mutual friends; (c) is attractive but a crime; (d) is poor form: he has after all met you socially without any prior consideration of what to him is the important question of your religion/ethnicity. The slightly longer answer is therefore (b): it saves embarrassment. But if you thought "carry on for the rest of the evening as if nothing had happened, stay cordial and then make sure you never set eyes on the schmuck again," award yourself a bonus point.

---

the nationality, race or religion you are about to slander with the word "black" or the word "Jew": if it sounds like racism when applied to them, it probably is racist and should not be used.

Disparagement of other races, nationalities and creeds should be avoided not only because it may cause offense, nor yet merely because it violates the precepts of political correctness and equal opportunity. The real problem with such prejudice is that it is intellectually flaccid. A racist is someone in the unhappily low condition of having to postulate someone inferior to himself.

YOUR FLY IS OPEN

Euphemisms have their uses and can be amusing. "The door is open but the beast is still asleep inside the cage" may get a laugh in standup, but in social situations it is easier and less embarrassing just to say "Check your zipper" or "Your fly is open." (The latter should be delivered matter-of-factly, not in the manner of one who has just discovered a still-warm cadaver.)

Similarly, an obstinately clinging booger or food particle does not need to be pointed out any more explicitly than by a quick "Wipe your nose/chin."

AFTERWORD

"Another etiquette book? Who needs it?"

"Everyone."

The author would say that, wouldn't he? But most works on the subject are based on the assumption that good behavior is informed principally and perhaps exclusively by the conduct of patricians. When Emily Post and Eleanor Roosevelt were calling the shots, they turned, consciously or unconsciously, to Washington, DC, for their models.

But not everyone hangs out in the capital, and after the Clinton impeachment, the Oval Office and the adjacent corridors of power seemed more blue movie than Blue Book.

So, let down by government (possibly not for the last time), we look elsewhere for good examples. But the search need not take us far; we find them all around us, and within ourselves.

Everyone is concerned to give a good account of himself; very few people — regardless of race, color, class, creed, ethnicity, you name it — go out of their way to create hostility. They just want to avoid embarrassment: causing it or feeling it.

And that's what this book aims to help you do, not by strict codification (the author's no Moses), but by suggestion and discussion. You might not agree with everything it says, but if it works as a sounding board, it'll have done its job.

INDEX

OTHER ULYSSES PRESS BOOKS

Fit in 15: 15-Minute Morning Workouts That Balance Cardio, Strength and Flexibility
Steven Stiefel, $14.95
Details a unique, full-body fitness program that even the busiest person can work into a morning schedule. The fun and flexible "7 days/7 workouts" plan lets readers choose from 55 specially designed 15-minute workouts.

Golf at the Top with Steve Williams
Steve Williams & Hugh de Lacy   Foreword by Tiger Woods, $14.95
Written by the most successful caddy of all time, this book tells how to get into a cycle of constant improvement and ride that cycle to lower scores.

The Golfer's Guide to Pilates
Monica Clyde, $14.95
Uses Pilates' combination of strength, flexibility, balance and mental focus to lower your score and improve every aspect of the game.

Jesus and Buddha: The Parallel Sayings
Marcus Borg, Editor   Introduction by Jack Kornfield, $14.00
This book traces the life stories and beliefs of Jesus and Buddha, then presents a comprehensive collection of their remarkably similar teachings on facing pages.

Mapping the Memory: Understanding Your Brain to Improve Your Memory
Rita Carter, $14.95
Helps readers reach a higher level of understanding about memory and how they can improve the working of their own brain function in this area.

Plyometrics for Athletes at All Levels: A Training Guide for Explosive Speed and Power
Neal Pire, $15.95
Provides the nonprofessional with an easy-to-understand explanation of why plyometrics works, the sports-training research behind it, and how to integrate plyometrics into an overall fitness program.

Workouts from Boxing's Greatest Champs
Gary Todd, $14.95
Features dramatic photos, workout secrets and behind-the-scenes details of Muhammad Ali, Roy Jones, Jr., Fernando Vargas and other legends.

To order these books call 800-377-2542 or 510-601-8301, fax 510-601-8307, e-mail ulysses@ulyssespress.com, or write to Ulysses Press, P.O. Box 3440, Berkeley, CA 94703. All retail orders are shipped free of charge. California residents must include sales tax. Allow two to three weeks for delivery.

ABOUT THE AUTHOR

After 25 years observing what the English-speaking peoples regard as good manners, Henry Russell decided that notions of etiquette are too often based on the false assumptions that it is a top-down practice and that proles, if they know what's good for them, should model their behavior on that of patricians. In fact, blue-collar workers have as much to teach bluebloods as vice versa, because both are equally concerned with avoiding embarrassment and offense.

A child of the Sixties, Henry Russell was educated at Oxford University and lives in London, England.